Meanings of Modernism: Form, Function and Metaphor

Introduction

The essays collected here are edited transcripts from a series of eight lectures entitled "Form, Function and Metaphor: Issues in Architecture" presented at Walker Art Center in Spring 1981. The series was part of an ongoing multidisciplinary education program, *Meanings of Modernism,* funded by the National Endowment for the Humanities Learning Museum Program. Lecture series are offered on specific themes in 20th-century art and related social changes, scientific and technological discoveries and historical events of this century.

Architecture is ideally suited to this kind of analysis, for it, more than any other art form, directly and daily affects the way we live, work and play. The built environment reflects and, in some instances, determines the social order and institutions of any culture: its history and aspirations; customs and rituals; economic and political systems; and its geography, resources and technology.

Some of the most heated debates concerning the meanings of modernism have taken place within the field of architecture. Modern architecture's rejection of the past and historical continuity, its search for universal form, its embrace of industrial materials and technological possibilities, and its neglect of local and regional circumstances, however well intentioned, created a set of problems that contemporary architects have been attempting to solve in the last two decades. Questions of what to do about limited energy sources, expanding world population, new technologies, dying cities and the quality of private and public life need to be addressed by the contemporary architect and the public in light of the successes, failures and miscalculations of much recent architecture.

It was not the purpose of the "Form, Function and Metaphor" series to enter into the post-modern versus modern scrap. The purpose was to identify and air, for a general audience, some of the aesthetic and social issues that everyone, architects and public alike, ought to be thinking about. How do patterns of living and architecture intersect? Can we have beautiful design that is affordable and energy efficient? What makes a building or neighborhood work? How does architecture affect human behavior? What makes cities livable? What can be learned from history and vernacular architecture? And, how does architecture work as symbol, image, metaphor?

We invited eight architects, art historians and researchers representing a variety of viewpoints and geographic areas to speak about issues that they believe are important for architecture today: social responsibility, human scale and diversity were among the constants throughout the series. Emilio Ambasz conceives of architecture as an act of the myth-making imagination. In this pursuit, he uses primal shapes, essential gestures and irreducible longings to create an architecture that is an indivisible part of mythology. And in a similar vein, Stuart Cohen, co-curator with Stanley Tigerman and Rhona Hoffman of the exhibition "Late Entries to the Chicago Tribune Tower Competition," discusses the skyscraper as icon.

Grant Hildebrand poses the question, "Can utility provide meaning *and* pleasure?" and answers it by citing an American tradition of practicality in architecture which he sees in the works of Richardson, Sullivan, Wright and Bel Geddes. He refers to Jay Appleton's *The Landscape Experience* which suggests that the value of the practical is not entirely practical—it may in fact have subtle and deep-running ties to issues of pleasure.

The development of a solar access policy has been the subject of Ralph Knowles's research since the early 1960s. In his essay he demonstrates the importance of sunshine for the spatial and temporal orientation of city residents. He discusses how we can have aesthetically diversified and satisfying design by working within the limitations of regulations that guarantee solar access.

Spiro Kostof also believes that people ought to be involved in the development of their environment. He traces the history of city planning through a discussion of Haussmann's Paris and Mussolini's Rome. He warns against what can happen when politicians and architects try to impose total schemes without regard for the cultural history and evolutionary nature of cities.

Charles Moore discusses the necessity of making people the center of the world through architecture. He cites his own projects—St. Matthew's church in Pacific Palisades, a town plan for Roanoke, Virginia and a park in Seal Beach—where the design process was open to the participation of the users in the belief that architects don't need to "educate the people" but need to learn from them.

Oscar Newman addresses the problem of how to create high density environments that serve the interests of the residents. He stresses the need for statistics and hard information about how human behavior and interaction are affected by building design.

Bernard Rudofsky professes that architecture, particularly domestic design, needs to intersect with patterns of living. In this respect, Western culture has a great deal to learn from the Orient. He would have us radically change the way we design and use our floors, bathrooms, beds and chairs.

Obviously, "Form, Function and Metaphor" raises many more questions than it attempts to answer. However, one of the primary intentions of the lecture series and its subsequent publication is to generate the interest and participation of the layman in contemporary architectural issues. The diversity of topics and styles allows the reader entry into the many ways in which architecture and design influence the way we conduct our lives. It is hoped that, at the very least, this *Design Quarterly* will provide the reader with a concise anthology of recent American architectural thought.

Melinda Ward, Director
Learning Museum Program

Beyond Metaphor,
Before Form

Emilio Ambasz
with Robert Hart, M. Mattei, N. Salvarani
Drawing for a House for a Couple
outside Cordoba, Spain   1979–80

Emilio Ambasz

I have a confession to make. I'm not Emilio, I am Ambasz. In reality I am Emilio's metaphor. I asked him to join me in this assignment, but he has excused himself on the basis that he is not a theoretician or an ideologue as are some of his European friends whom he unkindly calls "yesterday's Marxists, tomorrow's black marketeers." He claims that he is not interested in politics or in power as are some of his New York friends. But I don't believe it. He says he doesn't seek to make metaphors, but tries to create an essential image. He doesn't care to suggest models but rather he seeks primal images. And he conceives of architecture as an act of the myth-making imagination, a difficult pursuit to establish in any systematic way.

I've asked him to give me something that will explain to people what he does. Something from HIM, not my interpretation of what he is doing. He gave me two statements, actually two fables, one for the beginning and the other for the end of this essay. Emilio is speaking:

Members of a very large corporation came to me explaining that they were interested in investing some of their assets outside of their traditional field of activity. They wanted to invest in housing. They asked me to develop designs and a program with a view toward establishing a factory that would produce prefabricated houses. They provided ample research and development funds and the professional fee was agreed upon. The first step I took was to create a catalogue of domestic places which was organized into two sections: retrospective and prospective.

The retrospective section was conceived as an operation of the memory. It was a kind of historical recollection of domestic places, those fragments of the house that had survived the decay or the evanescence of their original context.

So the catalogue contained Pompeiian atriums, Japanese terraces, ambulatories, patios, courtyards, medieval window seats, Roman baths, roof gardens, arcaded porches, foyers, entrance halls and more. The prospective section was intended as an exercise of the imagination. It involved designing new places without any historical antecedents, and it postulated new spatial concepts that corresponded to emerging notions of flexibility, adaptability, territoriality and individual privacy. Now each of those places, those that were recovered as well as those that were postulated, was printed on a double page in the catalogue. On the left-hand page plans, sections and elevations were drawn, and on the right-hand page there was an axonometric drawing of the place. In the case of the retrospective section photos were added that were ever so slightly blurred so as not to fully reveal texture, while still denoting space and mass. Once the catalogue was completed, I proceeded onto the experimental stage. The goal was to test the capability of the proposed housing method to provide housing needs, not only those of a very large number of users of similar social and economic backgrounds, but also those housing needs of small groups with differing backgrounds.

In California we found 14 families interested in jointly developing a housing project for which they purchased a piece of land. Each family was given a copy of the catalogue of domestic places and each individual in the family was asked to make a selection of elements for his new home. Once the family members had completed their preliminary selection, they then sat down to discuss their choices with an architect of the group. Next the architect's task was to encourage the family to combine into a coherent scheme those elements that each member had selected. So they added places that had been overlooked and removed others when it became clear that they were incongruent with the central purpose of the group. The combination of things was sometimes bizarre but the experimental design team did its best to help each family to achieve a scheme that satisfied the programmatic and social requirements of the family as well as the psychological needs of every family member. Next they elaborated each family's housing scheme into diagrammatic plans, sections and elevations. Each dwelling was then sent out for bids and sub-contracted to builders of the area. The builders were not given working drawings nor details. Each contractor was expected to work them out according to his own building techniques and according to available materials.

Construction proceeded as smoothly as you can imagine with 14 different owners looking over the contractors' shoulders, but the builders managed to produce a house more-or-less on time and more-or-less within budget. Now, I have to confess that the so-called Pompeiian atriums, Dutch gardens and Corbusian roof gardens lost some of their texture when translated into the California vernacular. But the spaces were there all right and the juxtaposition of fragments, those fragments recovered from different historical periods, sometimes generated unintended ironies. They were nevertheless also suggestive of new meaning. The most important thing is that the cost per square foot of each house is about the same as the cost per square foot of the most inexpensive prefabricated system in existence, one that

is very rigid in comparison with the one that we developed. So we felt that we had managed to demonstrate to our satisfaction that it is possible to have a participatory approach to industrialized housing. However, since this approach did not require new factories or any new investments, we were fired.

A project that Emilio has been working on since 1973 is on a very beautiful hacienda site 20 kilometers outside of Mexico City. The people who bought it do computer programming for government and industry. They had in mind a development of office buildings. They employ 160 people: economists, mathematicians and programmers. Each of them is a prima donna and each of them had to have a window.

What Emilio proposed to them was a building that would take into consideration the fact that Mexico was a lagoon before the Spaniards came. Consequently, if you are going to build in Mexico and put a finger in the earth, you get water. So he proposed to build a basin hidden behind two walls. One of the walls is an energy wall—a sun wall—the other one is a billboard. The basin is approximately 450 by 450 feet and contains a power station where solar energy is turned into electricity at a horrendous price. The primary feature of the project is that every one of the components is ready-made—off the shelf. The offices are 50 by 50 foot barges which can be rearranged according to the needs of various programs and projects. The barges float until located in position. They're moved by a small motor boat, but once positioned, compartments are filled with water so the barges slowly sink four feet to the bottom where they rest. The polyethylene tubes connecting the barges are made by a French company, and are nine feet in diameter, with a movable floor on which you can walk. Under the floor are the coaxial cable and electrical wires that connect to the computer. A cloud of cold water mist, first used at rodeos to settle the dust and bring down the temperature, is used to make the basin's water recirculate, reducing the ambient temperature on top of the computer center, thereby reducing the air conditioning load. I believe that Emilio used the mist in order to produce a rainbow.

6

The main notion of the people sponsoring the construction of the building is that they may become a technocratic alternative to the present political system, and in case a revolution comes, they may be appointed as the new priests of power. Now, Emilio insisted that there was no need for this building, that in reality all of these people could be at home with little terminals at their tables, but the employers were skeptical, so that notion is perhaps for some future time. The barges may be removed and one of the barges may be turned into an island of flowers in the Xochimilco tradition.

In an exhibition of Italian design that Emilio produced at The Museum of Modern Art in 1972, he again went to extraordinary lengths to make things look as if they had been taken out of a catalogue. By the end of the 1960s Italy was an interesting place in terms of design, not only because of its production of consumer goods, but also because of its high level of critical observation of the consumer society. The exhibition was divided into two parts: one part was environments that were shown inside the museum; the other part was presented in the garden and consisted of boxes, made for shipment to other museums, that contained furniture produced in the previous decade.

After the success of that show, Emilio was asked by a group in Grand Rapids, Michigan, to design a new museum. He suggested that they shouldn't build a new museum for their collection, but that since they were in Grand Rapids, the American center of furniture production, it made more sense for them to create an exhibition center concerned with the notion of artifact production. He also suggested to them that they utilize an abandoned federal court building that was in the midst of deteriorating Grand Rapids. As a result, they bought the building for one dollar from the General Services Administration.

The proposal was to reverse the entrance of this rather handsome Beaux Arts building and put it on the back side for several reasons: one is that it brings back the French interpretation of the Italianate type of entrance, so that in the Italian way you enter through the courtyard; also, putting the entrance in the rear had the advantage of reinforcing the edge of the neighboring retail development area. So to some extent it helped to reinforce the process of downtown revitalization. It also related the building to the junior college in front of it, from which a great number of visitors to the museum would come. So Emilio proposed one simple gesture—an inclined plane. The inclined plane would lean on the building and would allow several things to happen: it would create a *porte-cochere* under which buses could come to unload their passengers; it would allow the creation of a stairway up to a grand foyer entrance; water cascading down the inclined plane and collected at the bottom for recirculation would provide air conditioning. This was also one way of lowering the heat load on the inclined plane. Furthermore there was a general notion of using an inclined plane throughout Grand Rapids in order to recover other buildings that could form parts of a community art center. There were two abandoned cinemas and one theater and the idea was to use inclined planes leaning in different ways on the buildings to indicate that any building with an inclined plane creating arcades or passages formed part of the art complex of Grand Rapids.

The next project was for a dormitory town of 3,000 inhabitants, about 12 miles from Hanover, West Germany, where many enlightened professional people live. The adults were concerned that the children, who did not, of course, remember World War II, should be given an object lesson relative to that war. They didn't know precisely what it should be, so they invited theologians, artists and sociologists to make suggestions.

Emilio proposed the creation of a number of gardens—relatively small gardens. A garden is assigned to each child born into the community. The gardens have an entrance composed of a wall and two trees

that lead into what is a contemporary notion of a labyrinth with no center. Each of the gardens is defined by walls of hedges, seven feet high, five feet wide, that define a walkway. The idea is that when a child is five or six years old he is taught the rudiments of gardening and becomes responsible for the plants, enabling him to begin to understand about cycles, about planning, about taking care of things. A further notion is that when the child grows up and wants to make a larger garden, he would have to negotiate with the neighbor and they would both have to cut their walls of hedges in order to expand the garden. The ultimate idea is that when the child, heavy in years and in wisdom, dies, the plaque of marble that bears his or her name is turned upside down and the garden is reassigned to a newly born. When that person is six or seven he receives the garden and must decide whether to respect the planting there or to uproot it. Now, of course, the townspeople are relatively sophisticated and they never thought that this idea would be realized, so there is a big plaque explaining that the townspeople who created this garden for their children do not believe that all the children will respect each other's gardens or that they will necessarily share them. But they hope that a majority will. There is also a clear awareness that some of the gardens will be abandoned or neglected, but that is a fact that was accounted for.

Emilio rather cynically thought he had won the prize because it was the cheapest building proposal but he was told that, while he might have thought he was being tongue-in-cheek, in reality his proposal was in the great Lower-Saxony tradition. You may recall that when the Hanoverian kings went to England from Northern Germany they brought with them their tradition that when someone goes into retirement, he is given a gift of a small plot of land.

Emilio Ambasz
with Robert Hart, L. Vinciarelli, R. Fontana,
R. Burda
Drawings for the Center for Applied
Computer Research and Programming
Mexico   1975

Emilio Ambasz
with Robert Hart, M. Mattei, N. Salvarani
Drawings for a House for a Couple
outside Cordoba, Spain   1979–80

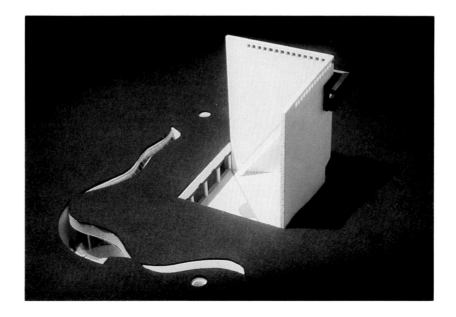

A recently completed project is a house outside of Cordoba, Spain. It's a house for a couple that sits in the middle of a marvelous wheat field. The house has an exterior stairway that ascends to a balcony. A handrail is excavated into the brick wall in such a way that it can carry water— water that cascades from the top where it originates its journey down to the bottom of the stairway where it makes a good deal of noise. You have a tremendous amount of noise in your ears as you begin the ascent, and as you get up to the top of the balcony it becomes quieter and quieter and quieter and the feeling is you have really arrived in paradise, because you no longer hear the noise of the water. The water that cascades down the stairway wall is recirculated. There are two stairways. They have been designed in such a way that only one can be used for ascension and the other for descent. The house is below ground.

In a curious way, this house is in the tradition of Spanish houses. A house in the south of Spain is always inwardly oriented. It looks onto a patio and has a colonnade and a cloister. Cordoba has a very arid climate and the temperature there can be quite hot, so with about three feet of earth above and a system of air circulation, the house can maintain itself almost throughout the year at about 68-70 degrees. There are two skylights and a little patio. The interior walls and the floor are covered with glass mosaics. There is almost no furniture. The main reason for the stairway wall is a practical one. It is oriented in such a way that the shadow is always on one side, and the balcony is always in shadow. Light that enters into the house enters by reflection from this wall. There is an alcove for sleeping, two bathrooms and a big sauna, closets, a kitchen, and another alcove in case of guests. The house is only about 1400 square feet.

Despite Emilio's Argentine birth, there is something very North American about his attitudes, about his distrust of the ideological and his apparent guileless predilection for simple truth. If he has any gift, it is that of stripping his formal production of the over-encumbrance of the kind of univalent ideology that has kept most visionary architects in a state of constant unemployment. Now Emilio, in opting to be a "fableist" rather than an ideologist, has grasped something very basic. Fables retain their ring of immutability long after ideologies have withered. For Emilio, the most creative and the most productive critical faculty is irony. If the work is sometimes compelling it is because it pretends that it doesn't compel. The invention of fables is quite central to his working method and it's really not a literary accessory. As we know, the sub-text of a fable is a ritual and it is to the support of rituals that his work has invariably addressed itself. It is at the level of distinguishing rituals that his projects perhaps make the most serious brushes with the reality of daily life. In the projects that we have seen, there is a paramount concern with the ritual organization of community. The users of his projects are usually small, self-contained societies, living in formal isolation from the larger social organization. This is the weakest part of his work. It would be interesting to see what he might do in an urban situation; undoubtedly he would surrender and sell out.

So far he has been careful to present his projects in rather special, very controlled, laboratory conditions. One of the projects of this nature is the cooperative for grape-growers in California. He posits a rather complex interrelationship between the ritual of growth and the harvest and the ritual of community building that actually takes place beneath the grape arbors. Another project of this type is the self-contained community of "farmers" in Georgia, again located beneath the matrix of agricultural production. Now in this case we don't have a leafy umbrella of grapes; what we have is really the land itself. The garden in West Germany is an exercise in pure ritual. All of these projects are essays in the ritual of dwelling and in the rites of the smallest of micro-societies—the family. The Mexican computer company, if we want to stretch the analogy, can to some extent be seen as a commentary on that most modern of social families—the company family. Now, if a certain flavor of arcadia penetrates his architecture it is with a most exquisite deliberation. As he himself has put it in one of his favorite aphorisms, and he is rather repetitive in them: "Europe's eternal quest remains utopia. The myth of the end. America's returning myth is arcadia. The eternal beginning." Now what arcadia is the central myth in Emilio's lexicon of cultural renewal? It's not exactly the commonplace arcadia of the standard dreams that we know. He elaborates a little bit further. "The traditional vision of arcadia is rooted in the humanistic garden, but America's arcadia has turned into man-made nature, a forest of artificial trees and of mental shadows." In his work, Emilio seeks to mingle the splendors of arcadia with those of the artificial trees and the mental shadows. As we have seen, it's not the machine in the garden that he is after but it's the machine and the garden. Or perhaps someone among you may say the machine under the garden. But while he may be suffused with Yankee visions of splendid nature, he is not suicidal. He knows that the machine is here to stay. It has become a part of us and there is no point in trying to subdue it or to conquer it, perhaps just to teach it its place, to make it show a little respect.

About ten years ago, Reyner Banham, in an attempt at rethinking architecture's use of technology, called attention to the diverse methods of environmental control which have been developed through the use of various sources of energy, and suggested the possibility that such new methods might perhaps provide new forms for architectural invention. While it is true that many of these ideas have lost their validity in the light of the present energy crisis, at the same time it was and still is a serious attempt at demonstrating that the architecture that we know is not the only possible one. Solar architecture constitutes a rather important step forward even if it hasn't meant, in most cases, anything more adventurous than adapting traditional building techniques for utilization of solar energy. Architectural concepts have remained the same. Perhaps there is the seed of an alternative solution in the work we have discussed as it abandons known and established materials and construction methods and the premises and design procedures which have been followed are not the ones that traditionally fit within the main body of architectural knowledge and experience. The building materials that we see in most of the work are either derived from the catalogues of high technology or they come from agriculture. Emilio calls it "agri-tecture."

Now he doesn't seek natural materials or utilize craft as a way of establishing an easy connection with tradition, but rather he wants to use different materials than those traditionally used in order to escape the narrow channels of established professional practice. He follows a procedure that might be called "bricollage:" the design of systems that are constructed with elements or with fragments that have been extracted from other systems that were created for a different purpose. It is a sort of metaphoric operation, where one word is made to stand for something else. But in this case that word or that fragment or that method or that piece of material is not made to stand for something else, it is brought in to a completely new context. Although the compositional methods are still architectural, the hope is that the result would not be the traditional type of architecture. Each of the elements, when detached from its original context, still retains its basic characteristics, but when introduced into a new context, it is reevaluated and is assigned new functions, new tasks and consequently acquires new meanings.

There is something critical that could be said about his selection of projects. One of the most basic criticisms that can be directed against him is that up to the present his work has been rather simple. But the simplicity, when it works best, is capable of producing objects of a certain emotional charge. Emilio has said that the only things he really cares for are pipes. The things that interest some architects, such as the art of architecture, the poetry, mean absolutely nothing to Emilio. He has hypnotized himself into believing that he has to attend to function because otherwise some of the things that he invents might overwhelm him and make him too self-conscious.

To close, he has written a second fable:

The little village was in the grip of fear—fear of divine rages and fear of human passions. One of the villagers started to build a structure that was circular in plan, cylindrical in volume and had a dome-like roof. He used stones and wood and mud. When he finished his work, he came back and told the group that the building he had erected was in the shape of the universe, and that inside the world was the god of the universe. Then taking a rod from the temple he made a circle around the village and with the help of the other villagers he encircled the village with a high wall which was built of earth and of stones. In the center of this village, next to the temple, he erected a large hut that he completely covered, except for the entrance, with a mound of earth. On top of this mound, he placed six vertical, stone slabs. This structure he called his home. The people in the village called it a palace. When he died, his body was laid down inside the hut together with all his belongings, and his son covered the entrance with the large stone slabs that he removed from the top of the mound. Some people say that this is the way architecture started.

The Skyscraper as Symbolic Form

Adolf Loos
Drawing for the Chicago Tribune Tower
Competition   1922

Stuart Cohen

The skyscraper was both the earliest icon and the last bastion of modern architecture. It provided modern architecture with its image of utopia—the city of towers. The technological history of the skyscraper from its beginnings in Chicago with the development of steel frame has been well chronicled. Revisionists have even suggested that the forms made by the architects of these early skyscrapers were expedient rather than ideological, as the historians of modern architecture wished us to believe. Because histories of modern architecture have dealt predominantly with the connection between the skyscraper and the development of technology, an entire period has been neglected—that of the eclectic, Beaux Arts skyscraper with its explicit ornamental and symbolic program.

Architects of the earliest tall commercial buildings addressed the aesthetic question of height by proposing that the "skyscraper" be seen as a composite—a series of proportionally related buildings stacked one on top of another. Each vertical layer formed a plinth on which the next layer sat in what A.G. Hyde described as the "heaping-up method" in an *Architectural Record* article of 1900. Another approach was to extend the parts of a conventional building base, *piano nòbile,* and attic, so that each became multistoried. Romanesque arches were stretched vertically as in George B. Post's Union Trust Building in New York City (1889-1900). Giant orders were employed in an attempt to solve the visual expression of the skyscraper within the ornamental system of traditional architecture. In each

case the visual logic of a form was extended. Along with Romanesque and Italian Renaissance, French *fin de siècle* architecture was employed and mansard roofs, that once maintained the Parisian cornice line while gaining another usable story, grew to contain four or five floors, as in Richard Morris Hunt's Tribune Building (1873-76).

The extended palazzo-type skyscraper, in which the *piano nòbile* could no longer pretend to be a giant space, may have suggested the metaphor of the column consisting of a base, shaft and capital. This theoretical solution is discussed in the writings of Louis Sullivan, John Root and the critic Montgomery Schuyler. In "The Tall Office Building Artistically Considered," Sullivan wrote: "We must now heed the imperative voice of emotion. It demands of us, what is the chief characteristic of the tall office building? And at once we answer, it is lofty." Sullivan's tall buildings, the Wainwright and the Guaranty, express his idea of loftiness by totally suppressing any evidence of the building's horizontal floor structure. Where historians like Giedion and Pevsner saw Sullivan's work as structurally expressive, in reality the columns of the Wainwright and Guaranty buildings were treated exactly as the vertical mullions separating windows. The entire upper portions of these buildings were fluted vertically; they were intended to allude to the column shafts. In Sullivan's tall buildings he took the idea of the column and coupled it with his own system of floral ornament,

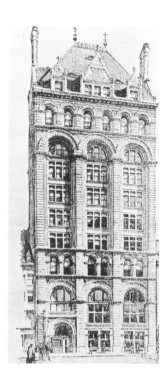

George B. Post
Drawing for the Union Trust Building
New York City   1889–1900

Richard Morris Hunt
Drawing for the Tribune Building
New York City   1873–76

based not on the *art nouveau* as historians have suggested but on his reinterpretation of Romanesque ornament. He wrote, "To my thinking, however, the mass composition and the decorative system of a structure such as I have hinted at should be separable from each other only in theory and for purposes of analytical study . . . a decorative structure, harmoniously conceived, well considered, cannot be stripped of its system of ornament without destroying its individuality." The inseparability of ornamental system and building suggests a column/tree metaphor. This is born out by the eruption of the cornices of Sullivan's skyscrapers into leafy ornament.

Most of Sullivan's contemporaries chose to work with far more explicit and codified historical systems of ornament. They worked, not by metaphor, but, by transforming specific European towers and church spires which they selected as precedents and models. Gothic church spires offered a more accessible congruence of ornamental program and meaning for the skyscraper than did the column, tree or vine. In the 1840s A.W. Pugin promoted Gothic as a religious architecture. "I must beg, in the first place, to draw your attention to the *use* and *intention* of spires. They may be considered under two heads, *natural* and *symbolical*. The natural use of a spire is as a covering or roof to the tower, the symbolical to make that roof an emblem of the Resurrection and to elevate the great symbol of our redemption. . . . The vertical line illustrative of the great mystery of the Resurrection is the very foundation of Christian architecture. Everything tends upwards and runs into pyramids and points, arches, roofs, vaulting, pinnacles, turrets, and towers. When the vertical principle was lost, Christian architecture soon declined, and four-centered arches, flat roofs, and square topped towers came in." Violet Le Duc the other great 19th-century proponent of the Gothic was an atheist who stressed its structural aspects in his advocacy of Gothic style.

In 1913 when Cass Gilbert's Woolworth Building was completed it was the tallest building in the world. Vincent Scully writes of its " . . . splendid continuity between mass and tower, sanctified by medieval quotation. . . . The semi-Gothic piers are as if bound together, and they lift in bundles of force from sidewalk to spire." A contemporary description saw it, " . . . bathed in electric light as with a garment, or in the lucid air of a summer morning piercing space like a battlement of the paradise which St. John beheld, it inspires feeling too deep even for tears . . . The writer looked upon it and at once cried out 'The Cathedral of Commerce' . . . "

The critic Montgomery Schuyler believed the success of the Woolworth Building's Gothic details would reopen the "battle of the styles." The most important event with respect to the question of the skyscraper's visual expressions, the battle Schuyler predicted, was the international competition held by the *Chicago Tribune* newspaper in 1922 for the design of its new office tower on Michigan Avenue. The program published by the *Tribune* as part of its competition made the symbolic requirements very clear: " . . . it cannot be reiterated too emphatically that the primary objective of the *Chicago Tribune* in instituting this competition is to secure the design for a structure distinctive and imposing—the most beautiful office building in the world." Clearly, the entrants in this competition, which drew 281 submissions from around the world, were being asked to design a symbol of the *Tribune*'s power and importance. The *Tribune* subsequently published a catalogue of all the entries to its competition and organized a traveling exhibition, " . . . for the stimulation and encouragement of better designs in skyscraper architecture, its appreciation by the public, and the consequent achievement of beauty in big buildings. . . ." The editors wrote that, " . . . the competition has achieved in a noteworthy way not only the *Tribune*'s purpose to procure for itself the most beautiful and distinctive building, but its secondary objective to stimulate architectural genius and bring forth works of beauty. . . . They [all the design entries] may be considered an encyclopedia of the architecture of the skyscraper."

Howells and Hood
Drawing for the Chicago Tribune Tower
Competition 1922

Cass Gilbert
Woolworth Building
New York City 1913

Eliel Saarinen
Drawing for the Chicago Tribune Tower
Competition 1922

The winning design by Howells and Hood was a Gothic tower that some critics felt was less successful than the second place entry from Finland submitted by Eliel Saarinen. Louis Sullivan wrote a critique in *Architectural Record* comparing the winning *Tribune* design by Howells and Hood to that of Saarinen. "One glance of the trained eye and instant judgment comes; that judgment which flashes from inner experience, in recognition of a masterpiece. The verdict of the Jury of Award is at once reversed, and the second prize is placed first, where it belongs by virtue of its beautifully controlled and virile power . . . it goes freely in advance, and with the steel frame as a thesis, displays a high science of design such as the world up to this day had neither known nor surmised." Why is Saarinen's design a work of genius? What was it about Howells and Hood's project that drew Sullivan's disdain? Sullivan continues, "Confronted by the limpid eye of analysis, the first prize trembles and falls, self-confessed, crumbling to the ground. . . . Starting with false premise, it was doomed to false conclusion. . . . The predetermination of a huge mass of imaginary masonry at the top very naturally required the appearance of huge imaginary masonry piers reaching up

from the ground to give imaginary support. . . . If the monster on top with its great long legs reaching far below to the ground could be gently pried loose, the real building would reveal itself as a rather amiable and delicate affair with a certain grace of fancy." A comparison of the two projects suggests that the most prominent difference, the one that Sullivan found unacceptable, was the application of Gothic forms—particularly at the top of the Howells and Hood design with its flying buttresses and "great long legs." Sullivan was denouncing the use of eclectic forms as he had denounced the Neoclassicism of Chicago's 1893 World's Fair. In spite of his own eclectic use of Romanesque architecture, the *Tribune* competition's cannonization of the Gothic style as the proper form for the skyscraper clearly went against his beliefs. Overlooking its Gothic details, the winning entry with its "certain grace of fancy" is remarkably similar to Saarinen's project. Like Sullivan's own Wainwright and Guaranty buildings these two Tribune designs almost totally suppress the horizontals of the building's floor construction. Windows are grouped between continuous piers making the visual expression entirely vertical.

Clearly the symbolic program of the American skyscraper had moved beyond the capacity of Sullivan's simple architectural metaphor. A Gothic skyscraper rose in Pittsburgh—the "Cathedral of Learning"—a university housed in a skyscraper with presumably clear symbolic meanings. Raymond Hood's project for the Central Methodist Episcopal Church of 1927 for Columbus, Ohio, raised a skyscraper above a cathedral and Holabird and Roche's Chicago Temple Building of 1923 placed a cathedral atop an office tower 550 feet above Chicago. It was within the capacity of the ornamental system of the Gothic skyscraper to satisfy the expressive and the symbolic requirements of structures that scrape the skies and reach to the heavens. It is this symbolic program and the images that were used to support it that link the "city of towers" and the "city of tomorrow" to

Le Corbusier
"The City of Tomorrow,"
from *Voisin Plan for Paris*   1925

A.N.W. Pugin
Churches from the *Apology for the Revival of Christian Architecture in England*   1843

Hugh Ferris
"The Four Stages," from *Metropolis of Tomorrow*   1929

Gothic images of the New Jerusalem such as the background of the Ghent Altarpiece, Jan van Eyck's *Adoration of the Mystic Lamb,* or to the city of spires illustrating the churches of Pugin from his *Apology for the Revival of Christian Architecture in England* (1843).

While the ornamental and symbolic program of the skyscraper came together in the Gothic tower, other skyscraper forms may also be understood in mythic terms. The romantic drawings of Hugh Ferris present a sublime vision of the skyscraper as a natural phenomenon. In his drawing, "The Four Stages," the skyscrapers are seen as a skyline of craggy peaks and mountain tops—a visual parallel made explicit by the mountain ranges in the background. The visual metaphor of the mountain, the symbolic link between earth and heaven, is offered as a solution to the "setback" skyscraper. The New York zoning law of 1916 required buildings over a certain height to step back from the street at a prescribed angle, with only 25 percent of the area of the site in a tower of unlimited height.

In *The Sacred and the Profane,* a comparative study of myths, symbolism and ritual, Mircea Eliade writes, ". . . the mountain occurs among the images that express the connection between heaven and earth; hence it is believed to be at the center of the world. . . . All these beliefs express the same feeling, which is profoundly religious; 'our world' is holy ground *because it is the place nearest to heaven,* because from here, from our abode, it is possible to reach heaven. . . . In cosmological terms, this religious conception is expressed by the projection of the favored territory which is 'ours' onto the summit of the cosmic mountain. . . . This same symbolism of the center explains other series of cosmological images and religious beliefs. Among these the most important are: (a) holy sites and sanctuaries are believed to be situated at the center of the world; (b) temples are replicas of the cosmic mountain and hence constitute the pre-eminent 'link' between earth and heaven. . . . As for the assimilation of temples to cosmic mountains and their function as links between earth and heaven the names given to Babylonian sanctuaries themselves bear witness; they are called 'Mountain of the House, House of the Mountain of all Lands . . . Link between Heaven and Earth,' and the like. . . . The ziggurat was literally a cosmic mountain, the seven stories represented the seven planetary heavens; by ascending them, the priest reached the summit of the universe."

The complex of images suggested by Eliade as points of connection between the earth and heaven—mountains, ziggurats, pyramids and mountain tops as *acropoli* or sacred sites—serve to explain reoccurring formal themes that may be seen in the eclectic skyscrapers built throughout the 1920s.

Innumerable skyscrapers have been topped by pyramid or ziggurat forms—symbolic mountains touching the sky. In the Bankers Trust Building in New York by Trowbridge and Livingston the building's smokestack is carried out through the apex of its pyramid roof—the ascending smoke is a further symbol of connection between earth and sky. Bertram Goodhue's influential Tribune Tower design of 1922 is topped by a pyramid surmounted by a statue of Mercury, the messenger, a fitting symbol for a great newspaper. In direct emulation of Goodhue's design Holabird and Roche's Chicago Board of Trade building is terminated by a pyramid which raises the figure of Ceres, goddess of grain, high above the city.

Temples were equally prevalent as terminations for skyscrapers. The skyscraper as mountain offered its summit as a sacred precinct, the site for the construction of temples. In his *Metropolis of Tomorrow* (1929), Hugh Ferris's drawing titled "Reversion to Past Styles" shows a Greek temple atop a set-back skyscraper. The image that Ferris refers to as "piling Parthenons upon skyscrapers" is remarkably similar to Frank Fort's design for the Tribune Tower Competition of 1922.

Bertram Goodhue
Drawing for the Chicago Tribune Tower
Competition   1922

Holabird and Roche
Chicago Board of Trade
Chicago   1929

Hugh Ferris
"Reversion to Past Styles,"
from *Metropolis of Tomorrow*   1929

Frank Fort
Drawing for the Chicago Tribune Tower
Competition   1922

Among the other mythic elements of connection between heaven and earth is the "universal pillar," an *axis mundi* at the center of the world. The pillar connects "our world" with heaven as well as supporting the sky. In myths it is also a tree, a vine, or a ladder, often the one the god or gods ascended after completing their work on earth. While Sullivan had offered the column as a metaphor for the tall building, skyscraper designs such as Adolf Loos's Tribune Tower dealt directly with the form and symbolic meaning of the column.

By the beginning of the 1930s the skyscraper's flirtation with traditional symbolic forms had ended. The tower was stripped of its eclectic ornament, the latter replaced by "moderne" geometric patterns. Unornamented vertical piers rose throughout each section of a building's mass as in Raymond Hood's Daily News Building of 1929 or Rockefeller Center. The question of the building's termination against the sky was solved by successive setbacks as Saarinen had foreseen in 1922, and by the mid 30s the "streamlined" skyscraper had emerged as a new symbol of the future utopian metropolis. By the late 30s the city of widely spaced towers on a grid had supplanted Hugh Ferris's image of the city as sublime mountains and canyons. By the 1950s the symbolic aspects of the skyscraper, particularly its representation of technology, were transferred, in Mies van der Rohe's work, from the form of the skyscraper to its steel details. In Mies's 860-880 Lake Shore Drive buildings the curtain wall expresses the structure at the expense of varying the window module. In his later buildings, like Sullivan's office structures, the expression of the curtain wall suppresses any reading of the structure in favor of the dominant verticals of window mullions and curtain wall stiffeners. Coupled with a columnar base and a top visually defined by panels of louvers, Mies's buildings reestablished Sullivan's conception of the tall building and established a visual formula for the skyscrapers of corporate America. These skyscrapers were, as Sullivan had hoped, no more and no less than an abstract expression of their verticality.

The Significance of Usefulness in American Architecture

Albert Kahn
Ford River Rouge Glass Plant
River Rouge, Michigan   1922

● *Grant Hildebrand*

One can divide architecture into issues of use and issues of meaning; is there possibly a link between the two? Are there ways in which utility may have meaning or pleasure for us?

Jay Appleton, an English writer and landscape architect, puts this issue in an interesting light in his book, *The Landscape Experience* (Chichester: John Wiley & Sons, 1975). Appleton suggests that deep in time, in the evolution and survival of species as they emerged, there was a link between survival and pleasure, and pleasure was the first condition. By this Appleton means that if animal A likes to eat and animal B doesn't, animal A will survive and animal B will not. There are obvious parallels in mating and I suppose in a number of other areas as well. The essential point of Appleton's thesis is that it relies on the pleasure notion as a precondition of the survival function; pleasure is the basic ingredient and survival is the result. It's obvious that as human beings, we find pleasure or relief of discomfort in survival functions such as eating and reproduction, but Appleton finds other examples that relate to our environment. He deals primarily with the landscape, but I'm going to extend his point to architecture and particularly to American architecture.

Appleton identifies three repetitive characteristics that he says exist in all designed landscapes. He calls these "refuge, prospect and challenge." By refuge he means places to hide or to be secluded. I suppose the purest example is the cave. One can also feel this in a grove of trees or in any place where one can see but isn't seen. By prospect he means a meadow, an expanse, an open space that allows us to see the things we're hunting. As a species we have always hunted and the prospect allows us that means of survival, and we find pleasure in that experience. Challenge is a more difficult issue. By challenge Appleton means the notion of apparent risk, and it would be his argument that species that are prepared to take risks, or indulge in risks, are more apt to survive. That risk taking is a part of the pleasure phenomenon is demonstrated in the delight that we find in a ferris wheel, in crossing a gorge, or in walking along a precipice.

John Ruskin speaks of an early experience he had near his childhood home, that in Appleton's terms would make a great deal of sense. The experience involves a refuge, a prospect, a river and the hunting ground of a meadow beyond and perhaps as well the notion of challenge in the dramatic hillsides and the crags of the vista. Ruskin's is a natural landscape, but Appleton finds these principles repeated in the designed landscape. A rather elegant example is Stourhead, the famous English garden in which Appleton would argue that the refuge is in spaces such as those surrounding this pantheon-like building, or in the pantheon itself, a place to retreat within its colonnade. The challenge is in the bridges and walks along the water, and the prospect is, of course, the lovely English sense of the meadow, the man-made meadow that occurs in the landscape.

How does Appleton's idea relate to American architectural design? It relates to the American experience because of the particular condition of the European immigrant to this land and subsequently, our experience of westward expansion. The European who first came to this continent was the person who was willing to take on practical problems and challenges, survival processes if you like. And if one hadn't a taste for that kind of thing, one didn't come. One could argue that those who came here were those in whom the survival-pleasure link was particularly strong, and that Americans have that characteristic in special strength. (And in fact, our heroes epitomize that notion. One can draw easy distinctions between certain American and Greek heroes. They had their Ulysses and Achilles as we have Tom Sawyer, Wild Bill Hickok and Johnny Appleseed; but there is a difference, and I think it's a particularly American difference. Our heroes are not the ones favored by the gods, but the ones who tough it out. We don't know whether Hector or Achilles was the better warrior, we only know on whose side the gods intervened. But we know that Wild Bill Hickok was the fastest shot in the West, and that's how he made it, and the gods had nothing to do with it.) This emphasis on survival, coping with practicality, making do, finding ways, was true certainly in 1620 on the Mayflower, and probably in 1720, 1820, 1860 and perhaps in 1930. Whether it's true in the 1980s I don't know, but I do think that by this time it has become a part of ourselves, a visible tradition.

Does this tradition affect our architecture? Yes, it does. We've accomplished a good deal out of this predilection. Our energies are given to ingenuity, Yankee ingenuity, and it has made a difference.

Let me cite as one example the genesis of the American barn. One of the classic European barns is the tithe barn of Great Coxwell just outside of Oxford. It's a long, medieval barn all on one level with aisles running the length of the building, gutting its usable space. The American, the immigrant, coming from that same setting and making a barn, changed a number of things. First, the material: a document of 1720 records that one farmer " . . .tried stone at first and the animals got sick and

the accrual of frost on the walls contributed to disease." He goes on, " . . . wood would have been cheaper and easier and more healthy as well," and that's what the American used, overwhelmingly, as a choice material. The farmer also changed the barn's organization. His aisles, instead of gutting the heart of the building by running its length, were developed as cross-axes in the American model and he used a multistory scheme—more square footage per structure. The food goes above and the animals below. Sometimes one even finds a three-story barn, the lower floor being for fertilizer. It's what we might call utilization of gravity flow to serve agricultural productivity. It's a deployment of ingenuity addressed to the practical issues of farming that in some distant way explains why we are exporting grain to Russia today.

Practical invention does make a difference in our architecture; it changes our buildings. The balloon frame house is another example expressed in the attitude towards the usefulness of wood. You make it in little sticks so that you get more wood from saplings; no need to wait for the mature oak forests of England. You put it together with little nails instead of losing weeks and months making the carpentry joins of traditional European buildings.

In *The Architecture of the Well Tempered Environment,* Reyner Banham traces the emergence of technical controls for heating, cooling and so forth, in buildings. He says, "This story is largely a North American story. This is where it happened." Another example, even more powerful, concerns the Eiffel Tower. Built for the 1889 Paris Exposition, the Eiffel Tower was, by statute, to be entirely French. It was a symbol of French national pride. Yet the elevators were American Otis elevators and they still are. Because we could build elevators and no one else could at that time, our cities had tall buildings when the rest of the world did not.

Interior of the medieval tithe barn at Great Coxwell
Berkshire, England

Albert Kahn
Ford Motor Company Factory
Highland Park, Michigan   1910

In the architecture of industry there is a similar story. In the 1834 Amoskeag Mills of Manchester, New Hampshire, the notion of buildings as isolated artifacts has begun to disappear. They are seen as lines of process, grouped along the lines of movement of goods. Is this the root of the assembly line? Attitudinally it is the idea of seeing process as the heart of the problem. Albert Kahn, in the early 20th century, took a very decisive lead in architectural provision for the industrial process. Kahn's early factories were multistoried structures that depended on wall windows for light. This limited the building's width; it was the Gordian knot of industrial architecture at the turn of the century, which Kahn, in 1906, in the Buffalo, New York, Pierce Arrow plant, cut through. Kahn realized that with light from the roof a plant can extend horizontally, following the logical industrial process; the building can be what the manufacturing process wants it to be. The interior of the Pierce plant looks then oddly modern and oddly suited to the 20th-century mass-production process. It's rather surprising that the assembly line was never used here but appears in another building by Albert Kahn about seven years later.

In 1910 we get the first inkling of that sort of thing happening in American industry in the Highland Park plant that Albert Kahn designed for Henry Ford's Model T, that approaches the problem of process and assembly with a fresh point of view. All the raw materials come in at the top and drift down through chutes and through balconies to the bottom where they become the completed car. Ford and Kahn are toying here with notions of how to get the thing put together in a better way and what kind of architecture will do the job. And if you think back to the barn discussed earlier, the analysis of a problem here has some parallels in earlier American vernacular architecture. Remember, Henry Ford grew up on a farm.

In March of 1913 the assembly line process was first used for magneto assembly, and that turned American factories to one story, roof-lit schemes of the Pierce sort. So between Ford Highland Park and Albert Kahn's Pierce scheme, we have the seeds of modern American mass production architecture that by 1920 had manifested itself at the Ford Rouge plant. Ford saw the handwriting on the wall for this process in architecture, and he bought 2,000 acres on the River Rouge and began building there with Kahn as his architect in what was eventually to be the largest industrial complex in the world. Buildings at Rouge were almost without exception one-story roof-lit, steel-framed structures whose design was carefully tailored to assembly line production processes.

I have implied that this attitude toward industrial architecture was well ahead of the rest of the world. Was it really? In 1933, 11 years after the River Rouge plant was constructed, the *Journal of the Royal Institute of British Architects* published an entire issue on English industrial architecture. Everything that it illustrated was a multistory, concrete factory without even the gravity flow advantages of Ford's Highland Park of 12 years before.

Europe had no notion of what we had been doing for 23 years. In 1927 the Italian Fiat firm decided to put up a new factory that was going to be the most modern in the world. Yet Fiat, in 1927, five years after River Rouge, built an exact copy of Kahn's Highland Park plant of 1910. Everything is the same except they reverse the single advantage that Highland Park had, the notion of gravity flow. At Fiat, the raw materials start from the bottom and are manually hoisted up, and the finished product comes out on the top where it makes a sort of helix to get back down to the ground. Was American industrial architecture ahead of the world? It was ahead by decades.

I grew up on Norman Bel Geddes's book *Horizons,* published in 1930; I'm only now beginning to appreciate its significance for our history. Bel Geddes had a wide vision, and he redesigned an astonishing range of artifacts. Many of his schemes seem to our eyes outrageous. He designed an airplane to carry 400-odd passengers with a crew numbering in the hundreds. It had a cruising speed of about 100 miles per hour. This plane, quite far from being a Buck Rogers thing, was flyable and would in the end, perhaps, have been the only viable challenge to the ocean liner had it not been for the advent of the variable pitch propeller, and in later days the jet engine. The plane nevertheless was a scheme that in many ways addressed the technologies of its time. Bel Geddes also designed houses: in one example, the garage is very amusing. The car is driven in and onto a turntable; the turntable revolves so that the car can be driven out again without backing down the driveway. The house is also carefully considered in terms of appliances, including a dishwasher, a garbage disposal and a gas range that revolutionized appliance design. And so I guess the point I'm making is that naive as some of these things seem, they are nevertheless, in their way, tough attitudes towards practical issues in design.

Let's compare Bel Geddes's innovations with this more famous example by, of course, Le Corbusier: the 1929-31 Villa Savoy in Poissy. In Corbusier's terms, "the machine for living," but this house, in fact, in its appliances or its gadgetry or its notions of climatology, says nothing at all about the issues that Bel Geddes was trying to address. It's more beautiful in many ways than Bel Geddes's house, but a totally different attitude created it.

In European work one finds an infatuation with various forms of technology. Le Corbusier writes about the beauty of the American grain elevator and the American factory. He writes paeans of praise to the American factory including River Rouge, and László Moholy-Nagy of the Bauhaus illustrates dramatic pictures of Ford's Rouge, but neither of them bothered to understand things like the plan and section of the glass plant or what lay behind those seemingly crisp forms. Europe had a love affair with technology, redolent with romance, but without much consummation. American design, by comparison, seems to hop into bed with technology without much romantic preamble, and it gets things done. Why no manifestos in the U.S.? Why don't we find paeans here such as the futurist manifestos? Perhaps because the use of new technology was so much a part of us that we took it for granted. The useful was useful—not inspirational.

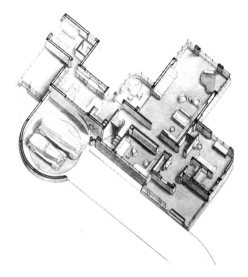

Norman Bel Geddes
Ground floor plan for House Number 3
1930

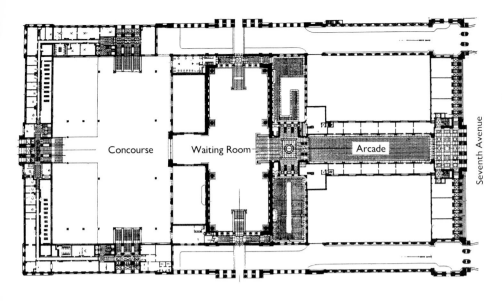

Seventh Avenue

Concourse　　Waiting Room　　Arcade

McKim Mead and White
Ground floor plan for Pennsylvania Station
New York City　1906–10

Now this point does not apply only to industrial architecture, and I don't intend to limit this essay to that issue. Let's examine a work by a firm that, at the turn of the century, represented the epitome of high style design: McKim, Mead and White's plan for Pennsylvania Station. Magnificent plan! Passengers come into a vestibule, past all the shops, marvelous access, straight through, down some steps to the waiting room, then out into the concourse; or one can come along with a carriage, or later an automobile, and with baggage in hand enter directly, without any stairs, into the waiting room and then to the concourse; or one can enter from the side streets, across a bridge down into the waiting room and to the concourse. Thoughtful sorting out of circulation systems, but where are the tracks? If you look at any railway station in London, the tracks are visible from the waiting room. Here the tracks are underneath. The whole problem of the noise and mess of the train and the problem of getting to the cars in safety is solved by tucking everything underneath. Again you might think of the American barn or the Ford Highland Park plant for the Model T. Thus Penn Station has a great deal of formal elegance, but nevertheless, it represents a

masterful grasp of the complex practical issues of a new age. Though it looks dated in its operational aspects, it is not at all. It is a magnificently studied building.

This practical tradition also underpins the careers of the great American triumvirate of Richardson, Sullivan and Wright, and I think it was one of the characteristics that gave them their titanic stature. Richardson's background was in the Boston waterfront and in tough problems outside the Ecole des Beaux Arts and he, in spite of the seeming stylistic elements of his buildings, cut through the mud of American design of his time to an understanding of design as material, volume and program, the reasonable expression of these things. There is more to Richardson than just style. He addresses the nature of building, of what architecture is. With Richardson, the column holds things up; an arch spans a void. I see in Richardson, too, this kind of tough practical approach leading to a very mature, magnificent sort of rebirth in late 19th-century architecture.

In Sullivan the case is crystal clear. In his essay, "The Tall Office Building Artistically Considered," he analyzes the program for tall office buildings: mechanical stuff in the basement, then two commercial floors, then tier on tier of offices and finally, he says, on top, " . . . the great turn of the mechanical systems. They make their grand sweep ascending and descending." The envelope is a poetic embracing of a very crisp and tough analysis of what this new building is. The Guaranty Building, as one mature example, is a poetic and rich working out of a hard-nosed analysis of program. And I especially love that top. The mechanical systems make their grand turn ascending and descending with the ornament, just hugging that form, pulling and twisting them over the top. Lovely termination. But if he had not understood the mechanical accoutrements, could the poetry have emerged? That's the

Adler and Sullivan
Guaranty Building
Buffalo, New York   1894–95

Adler and Sullivan
Interior detail (after 1960–67 restoration)
Auditorium Building
Chicago   1886–89

Frank Lloyd Wright
Robie house seen from the street side
Chicago   1909

integration that makes Sullivan a particularly American genius. The Auditorium Building is the first public building in the world to use electric lighting and mechanical ventilation. But they are not just used, they're poetry, they're ornamentation. Could this marriage between technology and art or practicality and form have happened elsewhere and isn't it this marriage that gives such a rich and timeless quality and significance to Sullivan's work?

The case of Frank Lloyd Wright, I think, is perhaps the most interesting of all. Reyner Banham has shown that Wright was a master of the integration of heating and ventilating systems. The heat was intended to be buried in the floor in the Robie house where, as we know was proper, it would bathe the outer walls and then rise and escape as ventilation through delicate grilles in the ceiling. In the summer, the air came in through a bank of French doors under the deep shading overhangs and across the cooling planters and out through the grilles. Or examine Wright's integration of electric lighting. How many designers make architecture of technical lighting systems? Wright had worked on Sullivan's Auditorium and he didn't forget the lessons. The early Wright houses, like Sullivan's Auditorium, are models of how to make design and poetry out of practical considerations. I'm not saying that these houses are only about practical considerations, but these are one source of the richness that they possess.

Wright's houses mingle use and meaning. In speaking about the Robie house and other houses of that time, he found satisfaction in the fire that burned deep within the heart of the house. He tends to bury that fire in innumerable examples; the Robie house, the Cheney house, or Falling Water, at Bear Run, Pennsylvania, where the fire burns within rock nests that bury themselves in the earth. Is this fire the cave fire? And is this the refuge? And are these balconies at the Robie house or Falling Water the prospects or meadows of Appleton's thesis? And do we have here a conjoining of those early survival experiential phenomena in which we originally found pleasure, and is this part of the richness we feel?

We have come, by a rather circuitous route, back to Appleton's thesis of survival functions as keys to a pre-existing pleasure, and through this to an awareness that the practical traditions of our architecture are in yet undiscovered ways possessed of meaning and pleasure. Architecture today is very much engaged in a search for meaning. One might almost say a frantic search. Architects are trying to discover meaning in form, and the post-modern period is trying to do this through analogies to linguistics and recollections of classic orders. But maybe the issue of meaning in architecture is both simpler and more profound, and is perhaps particularly suited to a realization or rebirth of an essential American contribution.

I believe that a distinctive characteristic of American designers is a predilection for and a skill in handling practical issues. It has shaped our design history. It has colored our attitude. It has determined the forms of our cities, for better and worse. It's been an important factor in the shaping of our particular surroundings and I have argued that it has in some degree had an impact even on architectural works that seem very much removed from this kind of thread: the work of McKim, Mead and White, or the shingle style of Richardson, Sullivan or Frank Lloyd Wright. It seems to me that their success relates to and is enriched by this thread or tradition. And the greatness of this work is, I think, integrally bound up with the presence of the American tradition. Our experiences and our attitudes, shaped through generations, make us a different people from our European forefathers, and the things that make our architecture rich aren't necessarily the things that have made European architecture rich. Although this is not the only way of understanding ourselves, I think it's a way that might possess genuine importance.

Solar Ethic, Urban Form

● *Ralph Knowles*

The sun's rhythm can be used as a design strategy. To understand this we must understand how we perceive our environment. In the 1950s, people like Kevin Lynch who wrote *The Image of the City* and A.E. Parr who talked about making cities in relation to our ability to understand them, voiced their concerns about a lack of diversity in our urban areas. Lynch was concerned with image, with legibility. We were in a time when our primary interest was to build a tremendous amount of volume and to do it as quickly as possible. We applied the techniques of industrialization to building. So it was not unreasonable to devise an aesthetic that was an expression of our understanding of industrialization. Multifolding, making things like other things: floor like floor, side of building like side of building; and finally, whole buildings like whole buildings. That assembly-line mode produced an image that bothered Lynch and Parr quite a lot. They felt it had very little to do with our ability to find our way around. We became, in Lynch's terms, "lost in the city." Knowing which direction was which, sometimes knowing up from down, became a real problem.

Parr made the point that we had adaptively evolved out of a natural rather than a man-made environment. That natural environment was differentiated. It was a world in which the tops of forests looked different from the bottoms of forests and what was in between was distinguishable from both top and bottom. Horizontal differentiation of the natural world was based on the depth of the water table.

Where the water was deep, a chaparral community was formed. Where the water table was shallow, a pine community was formed. Between them, a kind of edge, a tension zone was formed. It was from that kind of diversified world that we adaptively evolved.

In spite of the relatively undifferentiated character of our buildings, one surface looking like another, one building looking like another, the same kinds of forces act on them that act on the natural environment. Natural forms vary in response to that force differential, our buildings do not. And yet, if one examines incident energy on the faces of our cube-like buildings, it's soon discovered that different amounts of energy are received from one face to another at any given time; and over time, the amount of energy received will change. The amount of energy received in the winter is different from the amount in the summer. Our intuitions tell us a lot about general differences, but they don't tell us a whole lot about specific differences from side to side of building.

Our mode of construction following World War II didn't differentiate buildings. Instead it modified supplies of energy in such a way that we were able to overcome force variation simply by shifting energies, by controlling how much we used where and when. If we had differentiated building surfaces instead of amounts of energy, if we'd held the energies constant and varied building form, we might have ended with buildings that do not look the same from side to side. For example, sun screening might look quite different on the south

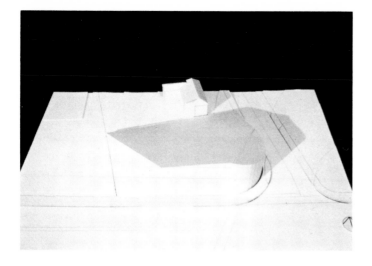

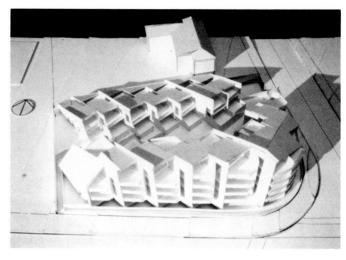

Moderate density housing project:
a) An envelope to the north of a major street slopes to the west, north and east to protect its neighbors (3 pm).

b) A housing design follows the envelope's contour while orienting each unit to capture the south sun in winter.
(Designer, Jeanette Quon)

Moderate density housing project:
a) Across the street, the 9 am shadows of an envelope match precisely to the outline of surrounding houses.

b) A housing design fits this second envelope so closely that its morning shadows are almost the same as those of the zoning envelope.
(Designer, Roy Murabata)

The application of solar design principles to urban building requires solar access. A zoning instrument that assures each site a fair share of sunshine is the solar envelope. The solar envelope is dependent upon the geometry of a land parcel and upon the period of desired sunshine. When, for example, six hours of sunshine (9 am–3 pm) are required on parcels of different size and shape, the envelopes will systematically vary. The envelope is thus a construction of time as well as space.

from that on the north and quite different again on the east and west. After reading Lynch and Parr, and James Marsden Fitch, whose *American Building: The Environmental Forces that Shape It* was one of the most influential books of the time, we began in 1962 to look at the possibility of adapting buildings to the differential effects of force. Not, as it turns out, primarily for purposes related to energy. At that time we were interested in the concerns of people who didn't want to get lost in the city, who, in fact, wanted to know which way they were going. We thought, if we could vary the shapes and structures of buildings, it would be possible to establish a sense of direction in cities. It would be a sense of direction growing out of the building's response to natural forces. We began to look at a kind of graphic response to natural forces. This graphic response is a sun control system. Underlying this system is a cube, and the rules of the game are very simple—to extend planes on a basic geometry just far enough to control the rays of the sun in some prescribed performance. The south face under those circumstances doesn't look like the east face. And if you take the same attitude about the top, neither face looks like the top.

The problem is that buildings don't usually stand in isolation. They stand in relation to their neighbors. Often, one building shadows another. That is so commonplace that it needs to be pointed out as a phenomenon of some consequence. For example, in Los Angeles it is possible that the sunny part of a building has to be cooled while the shadowed part has to be heated. If you think about the edge of a shadow as a demarcation between two different climates, the mechanical control problems induced by that condition become extraordinarily complex. Even if I design very conscientiously in relation to the sun, someone may come along and build a building next to me, making me look very foolish. It's not just a matter of casting shadows from one building to another; it's a matter of where and when the shadow is cast. This raises very serious questions related to the supply and control of energy, and ultimately to the broader and more fundamental issue of the quality of our lives. Why are we concerned with converting energy if it is not a matter of the quality of our lives?

In the Acoma pueblo, about 50 miles west of Albuquerque, New Mexico, buildings are terraced to the south and the streets run east and west. About 1968, we began a serious look at these pueblos in relation to their ability to convert energy by what has come to be called passive means, that is, to collect winter sun energy and store it and use it inside the building and to reject the summer sun energy. The reasons these mud and stone buildings act as well as they do are related to thermal mass, to transmission coefficients, to heat storage capacity. Let it suffice to say that they do work very well by exposing terraces to the south and especially to the low winter sun that strikes the wall masses of the buildings and by exposing roof surfaces to the summer sun—those roofs not having very much heat transmission capability and very little heat storage capacity. So as individual buildings their shape and their structure are well-adapted to the sun. They not only function well, but they have an extraordinary symbolic importance in the lives of the Acoma people. But, of course, the individual buildings don't exist in isolation. They exist in the context of a relatively small building group atop a plateau. Not much room to build a community with very high density and a limited technology. If the buildings are too close together, the winter shadow from one steps on the feet of the building to its north. So herein, apparently, lies a principle that relates the height of a building to its area of shadowing influence. In looking at this settlement on the sun machine, we could not find examples of major shadowing. Where they ran out of space and the street started to narrow, the buildings were made lower. Consequently, the relationship between height and area of shadowing remained more or less constant. It almost seemed as though they were practicing a solar ethic. A right to light. A sun right.

We became very interested in that principle and in 1976 began to work at converting the principle into a zoning tool. This is certainly not the only strategy for assuring solar access. There are legal strategies, such as permits, easements and covenants. What I'm describing here is a relatively straightforward strategy for zoning, a kind of uniform application of the relationship between the height of buildings and their area of shadowing influence.

In developing such a strategy for energy purposes it is terribly important to understand how many hours of the day useful amounts of energy from the sun are available. Summer and winter hours are different because the sun is generally higher in the sky for most of the day in the summer. If the critical angles of those varying times are transferred to a site it is possible to define the upper limit of developable volume that won't cast shadows onto a neighbor. The resulting volume is called a solar envelope. The definition of that solar envelope takes into account two basic premises: one is that you are not going to shadow your neighbor during critical sun times; the other is that you are going to provide the largest possible volume within those time constraints. Time constraints are not absolute. They can be adjusted. They can be modified to relate to different land uses, to different density requirements, to different climates and different latitudes. In Los Angeles the winter day is ten hours long and a summer day is fourteen hours long. In Minneapolis's latitude of 45°north, a summer day is sixteen hours and a winter day is only eight hours long. Obviously with those kinds of differences, time constraints must be adjustable. They can also be made to adjust to the needs and values of the community.

It's one thing to propose this sort of idea, it's another to understand the problems in it. So we began to test the idea of the solar envelope with very modest housing applications, but always in a real context.

Mixed-use project:
a) Large, mixed-use projects can have so variable a surround that the solar envelope will rise and fall in complex undulations that suggest land use within the site.

b) A design that follows the envelope's contours locates high office buildings at one end and lower housing at the other. A linking plaza is filled with winter sunshine but people can walk there comfortably under shaded arcades in summer.
(Designer, Randall Hong)

All of this work has been done in Los Angeles, beginning in a neighborhood of detached, single-family houses where two 50-foot lots have been put together to form a 100-foot frontage. The solar envelope defines the largest amount of volume that can be put on that parcel without casting shadows on surrounding houses during designated hours.

The designer's task is to capture the sun while retaining as much density as possible on the site. In our studies we began to be aware of the extraordinary way in which these designs responded in a rhythmic way. As the designers became more sensitive to the daily shifts of sun from east to west, and the seasonal shifts from north to south, the rhythms became a more important part of their designs. Rhythm began to emerge as a design strategy. In addition, there was the constant question, "Did the solar envelope interfere terribly with the property's development potential?" These two related questions are in every sense always part of the balancing act that concerns designers. So we kept pressing at density. We made a second study in Los Angeles, on Wilshire Boulevard, where a set of properties had lain vacant for quite a long time. There were expensive buildings in the surround. People who lived in houses to the north didn't want any construction on the unused properties, in fact, they wanted a private park there. Developers, of course, wanted to put 14-story buildings on the sites. The city planning director had a problem on his hands. Hearings were held. He put off a decision as long as he could. He heard what we were doing with solar envelope zoning, looked at our work and finally agreed that it was a rational approach. It was a way to stand in the middle, to build something that wouldn't make property owners too happy, but at least it wouldn't wipe them out. The developers, on the other hand, wouldn't be too happy either because there wasn't enough built, but it would give them something. And he finally did stand there. He solar-zoned the properties in the context of what is called in Los Angeles a specific plan, a piece of the city over which the planning department exercises considerable design control. In defining a developable volume on those parcels, it became evident that we were dealing with different potential on each side of the street.

I don't have to remind you that shadows cast from one building onto another are costing us a huge percentage of our energy resources every year, but setting aside the energy question, we are still confronted with the problems of quality. Scaling. We have cities that grow beyond our comprehension, beyond our ability to relate to them through perceptions that are adaptively evolved through millions of years. The buildings just get higher and higher. You can start out with five-story buildings and ten years later they are ten-story buildings. Ten years after that they are 20-story buildings and ten years after that they are 40-story buildings and ten years after that, or maybe five years, they are 80-story buildings. And of course the dimension of the streets never changes so what happens to the quality of life on the street?

From a design point of view, one of the things that is most intriguing about the solar envelope is its ability to scale new growth to old growth, to treat the old growth with some regard. It is—in the end—a designerly approach to zoning in which spatial aspects derive from the size and shape of pieces of land and of sites as they relate to neighboring buildings. But it is more than that. It's a definition of property in terms of time. Consequently, differences in our attitudes about time produce different amounts of volume. How we ask that volume to behave, to function, changes its form. When we begin to explore the limits of that form in design terms we are confronted with an aspect of time that we have not had to confront for at least a half century. We know that we can overcome natural differences by plugging in the system, we can ignore the time of the day by plugging in the system, we can bypass the difference between morning and afternoon, we can overcome the difference between summer and winter. Certainly there is something seductive about being able, by extraordinary expenditures of energy, to overcome the constraints of time and space, still it leaves something to be desired, and I'm not sure how much longer we can keep it up.

If we go back to the concerns of Lynch and Parr—scale our cities to our perceptions, scale what we build to our ability to understand, differentiate in ways that help us in finding our directions—then of course, we have got to do things in a somewhat different way. Solar zoning is one mechanism that begins to act as a frame within which differentiation in direction and time can take place. By the traditional mechanisms of location and form, architecture and urban design, we not only broaden the designers' palette but we make a richer kind of world. In a book called *Art and Technics* a number of years ago, Lewis Mumford wrote that choosing is a creative act. Yet, if one piece of the world looks like another piece of the world, there is no basis for choice. If one floor looks like another floor, if one side looks like another side, if one whole building looks like another whole building and if one street looks like another street, how do I decide? On the other hand, if by adapting the city to the same forces that work on us, have conditioned us, and to which we finally have to respond in the long term, we will diversify and provide a basis for choice. Most important, making that more diverse world isn't contrary to energy conservation. In fact, the two go hand in hand. If conserving energy by adapting our buildings produces a richer environment then we have a double gain. I believe that this is the design challenge of our time.

His Majesty the Pick:
The Aesthetics of Demolition

Spiro Kostof

One of the most characteristic self-created images of Benito Mussolini—alongside the fiery orator of the Palazzo Venezia balcony, the general on horseback inspecting the troops or parading at their head, the land tiller winning the grain war, and the paterfamilias surrounded by his wife and children—is the image of the Duce as wrecker, wielding his pick lustily on the roof of some structure in a condemned neighborhood. His own oratory and fascist literature in general are full of references to *il piccone risanatore* (the healing pick), and once in a speech of 18 March 1932, he refers to "his majesty the pick." For 20 years, between 1922 and 1942, radio and newsreels made of this humble implement a star, broadcasting its activities in the historic cities of Italy. The proof of this feverish work may be seen today in cities large and small from Genoa to Palermo.

These clearance projects were called *sventramenti*, literally disemboweling, taking the guts out of, making hollow. The word goes back at least as far as Haussmann's use of *eventrement,* and is part of that medical terminology that became common among administrators and planners in the early 19th century. It denotes that drastic cure, massive surgery, needed to save a badly infected urban organism. They are there still: those fascist thoroughfares out of scale with all surrounding urban tissue and vast inarticulate piazzas oozing space in all directions around an historic monument. And then, there are those thousands of photographs that have survived—the Duce's sole concession to the few people who complained of patrimony lost. They

are the hasty, semi-official record of what was demolished and they were usually taken when the buildings were already gutted and the shells stood haunting and lifeless, hollow window holes like gouged eyes, a carcass picked clean of life and memory. On occasion, the former inhabitants lined up for one final group photo in front of the place, the shell that had housed and reared them, where they played and fought and married, a touching portrait on the eve of their uncertain relocation to an alien, empty, memory-free new ambience. In annual reports, the proud account of all this labor would be entered, lists of streets and piazzas that had disappeared forever and statistics of housing units destroyed: 20,000 in Florence alone between 1927 and 1931, 60,000 in Genoa, 110,000 in Milan, and so on, interminably. It was fashionable then to destroy. The Duce was not alone. The rhetoric had been forged in the heat of World War I by the futurists, the spiritual forefathers of early Fascism, whose hate for old cities was indiscriminate. "Get hold of picks, axes, hammers and demolish, demolish without pity, the venerated cities," Marinetti urged. And Sant'Elia agreed. "We feel we are no longer the people of the Cathedrals . . . but of immense streets . . . of salutary *sventramenti.*"

(opposite)
Mussolini inaugurates clearance project of the Mausoleum of Augustus, Rome 22 October 1934

Demolition in process for Via dell'Imperio,
Rome   ca. 1930

Via dell'Imperio completed, seen through a
second-story arch of the Colosseum

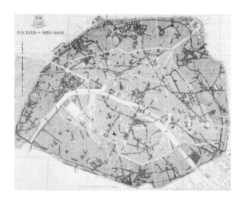

Baron Georges Haussmann
Plan of Paris   1854-89

With the birth of the modern movement, the incestuous, urban clutter of those culture-breeding European centuries was now derided and condemned in the name of scientific functionalism. Le Corbusier's Plan Voisin envisaged wiping out most of historic Paris. Oh, there were to be exceptions, of course. "The axis of the undertaking was well-chosen," he writes. "You can see the Tour Saint-Jacques which has been spared." The fanaticism may have been polemical, but the point of view it served was no joke. And it made the mid-19th-century vision of the Baron Georges Haussmann, for this same Paris, fainthearted by comparison.

Now Haussmann, the "demolition artist" as he was called by his detractors, was of course the great precursor of such pitiless, massive urban surgery. The city as a sleek efficient machine was his unacknowledged legacy to the modern movement. The scale of later fascist interventions, their worship of the straight line, monuments that float in seas of space, all this had Haussmann's actualized model to look back upon. Haussmann's treatment of Paris was in fact the first total conceptualization of what we understand by "the modern city." It heralded a technocratically minded, comprehensive approach to town planning in which a rationalized circulatory network would once and for all sweep away the dross of the community's promiscuous life through time. This overarching urban logic was revolutionary. It was the child of the new industrial-capitalist perspective and so was its guiding concept of obsolescence versus progress, applied now to what was beginning to be called "the urban plant" and its components in that mechanical analogy of the city that increasingly competed with the pathological.

But the aesthetic or expressive vehicles of Haussmann's *grands travaux* were themselves conservative. The wide and straight tree-lined avenues, the monumental vista, continuous uniform frontages, and the spatially profligate piazzas went back directly to Napoleon Bonaparte. And beyond Napoleon the Great were two centuries of Baroque experiment with the sweeping gesture, with a calculated public scenography and willful geometries. But Napoleon's planners had imposed something special on this cumulative body of urban

intervention and that is what is particularly relevant to the later Haussmann epic. This "something" falls under two headings: first, the still-embryonic notion that planning is a rational amelioration of public life, an effort that considers the grand visual dominion of proposed urban arteries and squares as the frame of coordinated systems of amenities and services: circulation, water supply, sewage, public order, business, entertainment, burial. This is one side of what is new in Napoleonic practice. The other is the willingness to countenance wholesale destruction of the cores of the very old cities of Europe, as demonstrated in the Napoleonic projects for the key stations of his empire from Brussels and Madrid to Milan, Rome and Cairo.

At the time of Napoleon, this new embryonic notion of what planning is all about, and this willingness to destroy the centers of historic cities, were not seen as convergent activities. On the one hand you had civil engineers and administrators who attacked planning in a systematic way, even to the extent of what we would call today regional planning. Their object was to address problems of health and traffic, to see physical design as a remedy for administrative, economic and social ills, or pressures. The anxiety of historic continuities, the assessment of built heritage, vistas and memories, these did not occupy them very much. It was, on the other hand, architects, people concerned with the art of civic design, with formal organization and symbolic presence, who proposed the great forums, the boulevards and *rond-points* in the thick of historic centers.

Destruction of entire sections of a city was condoned to make room for the public theaters of Napoleon's regime. These theaters were forced upon the old cities in order to reevaluate the monumental achievement of the past in relation to the new master of these old cities, to Napoleon himself. The presentation of ancient monuments in a drama of historical association brings out the comparable or rather competitive grandeur of the present regime in relation to the past. A century later, the fascist regime had the same idea.

Napoleonic plan for the enlargement of
the Piazza di Trevi, Rome   1809–14

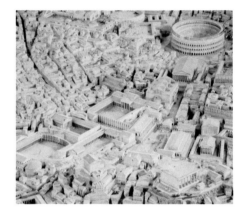

Model of ancient Rome showing
the Imperial Fora

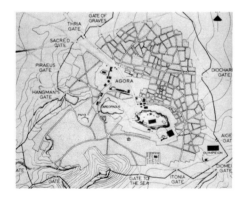

Plan of Athens showing the *agora*
5th century B.C.

Size, surely, has always appealed to autocratic minds, but earlier autocrats of the Baroque era had sought to gain their grand settings by planting them primarily in unoccupied or underbuilt areas. Versailles was not built at the expense of Paris. The breath-taking Roman avenues of Sixtus the Fifth go through vineyards and fields, on the edges of the historic frame of the city, yet within the city's walls. No pope of the 17th, 18th, or 19th century consented to the demolition of the spine in front of St. Peter's. In fact it wasn't done until the fascist period. Absolutism treaded cautiously when it came to built areas. Single monuments, yes. New facings, cartouches, propagandistic art, but not disembowelings. Not *sventramenti*. Napoleon's men were fearless. If the cavernous squares and heroic avenues they proposed had been realized, they would have upset, once and for all, the subtle spatial play between small buildings and large, monumental nodes and the standard tissue that gives these monuments their status, their impressiveness.

The only difference between the Napoleonic and the later work of Haussmann or Mussolini is that *they* saw traffic and glory as convergent goals. The boulevards that focused theatrically on historic monuments were also now meant to carry fast traffic smoothly through the once congested, near-impassable tangles of the city. The piazzas where monuments stood in their "necessary solitude," to quote Mussolini, doubled contradictorily as anchors of busy traffic junctions.

Looking further back, beyond Napoleon, and beyond the Baroque, for this enormity of puncturing gargantuan voids in the quick of aged cities, one earlier example springs to mind. It's the one that would of course have come to Napoleon's mind, quite consciously—Imperial Rome. We all know the drastic change that came upon the venerable capital of the Roman Republic when, beginning with Augustus, the emperors put aside its traditions of self-rule for a centralized government on the model of Eastern kingdoms. And no better instance can be cited for our present argument than the complex known as the Imperial Fora. This complex, created additively by a succession of emperors from Augustus to Hadrian, broke through the old walls of the republican city to marry

it with the entertainment quarter of the Campus Martius. There one of the great creations of antiquity was carved out to provide a spacious lung for the teeming crowds of the city which, in the time of Hadrian, probably had about a million inhabitants; the largest city that the ancient world had known. But this was achieved at the expense of existing serviceable construction, residential and commercial.

It was in the Hellenistic cities that preceded Imperial Rome where the idea of a city as a work of art, a design to be controlled and orchestrated, first emerged. I don't mean cities laid out all at once for an artificial purpose: colonial implants, military camps, or royal capitals that are born by fiat and forcibly populated. These of course all had regular designs, usually grids of some kind, that were abstract and repeatable. I mean cities that had risen more haphazardly, more organically, and now found themselves in the Hellenistic period untidy and congested with only a focus or two of monumental effort within their tangled and scruffy fabric. To give these old Greek cities the highlights of a self-conscious scheme, to run ceremonial axes through them, to monumentalize the approaches and cut into the shape grand formulas, theaters of public life—the Hellenistic planners had to demolish some of what was there, displace people and disrupt old habits as they enhanced and aggrandized. Sometimes the process was in the nature of a face lift. Creating unified facades through the addition of stone porticoes was one solution. These are the ancestors of Vigevano and Baroque Turin. But Hellenistic and Roman interventions were sometimes much more brutal. The change of the Athenian *agora* in the 2nd century B.C. is one example.

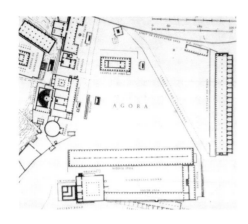

The *agora* of Athens after Hellenistic replanning   2nd century B.C.

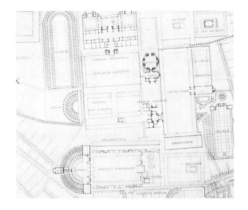

Plan of ancient Rome, Campus Martius area

Campus Martius area   ca. 1980

The point is not just the aesthetic change. Town planning is never innocent of political or social ends. The old towns had been self-governing entities. Everyone was theoretically equal, everyone's public life was of more account than his personal fortune. So, there was no question of avenues with fancy houses and public display of luxury, distasteful to a culture that equated beauty with morality. Public buildings were symbols of community; they were paid for with public funds and they served high-minded functions—religion, education, the institutional patterns of self-rule.

In the Hellenistic period urban self-rule is more a form than a reality. The rich live ostentatiously and donate public buildings that bear their names. Extra-urban powers, such as the king's, interfere with the structuring of the city fabric. We now have buildings named after individuals and in such conditions the poor and their buildings are expendable. They're forced to seek their pride in the endowed magnificence of powerful benefactors.

What of the long period between the collapse of the Greek or Roman world and the beginning of the Baroque? What of the Middle Ages and the Renaissance? The classical cities shrank drastically after the fall of the Roman Empire. Those cities that persisted adjusted their proud frames of Hellenistic or Roman times to the new exigencies of a minimal population, of a Christian society in vastly reduced circumstances. In the East something similar was happening. When Islam took over the already rather decrepit cities of the Greco-Roman world, it started to fit them slowly and without any elaborate premeditation into its own way of life. The colonnaded avenues that we admired in the Hellenistic/Roman world became the suqs (Muslim marketplaces) of later times. Individual bays were covered and made into shops, the whole line becoming rather raggedy and more human in everyday terms. And the great grids of the formal cities of the Hellenistic/Roman world were carved into by little alleys, cul-de-sacs, blind alleys, and so on, to form super-blocks, where tribal and ethnic groups could turn in upon themselves and ignore the abstract formality of the geometric grid. In the Christian West, too, the feudal fracturing of the urban form into defensive rival neighborhoods wrought havoc on the formal geometry of public ways. In Rome the great theaters, the stadiums, the baths, the public colonnades were cut up into little pieces. These vast structures were too expensive to keep, and culturally they were not compatible with the new religion of Christianity. They were fissured little by little into small-scale manageable tissue eloquent of survival and cultural reevaluation.

The concept of *civitas,* the assembly of citizens, came to supplant the more abstract, artistic notion of the Roman city or *urbs.* Isidore of Seville writes in the 7th century that what was more important now was " . . . not the stones, but the people." Now, it had been that way once before: the Athens of the 6th and 5th centuries B.C. had been small, moral entities where community was more important than setting. With the Hellenistic era had come the notion that urbanism was not the faith of public life, but the art of public living. And now, in the early Middle Ages, we are back again to a basic grouping and crowding that corresponds to the realities of daily existence, not to the lavishly subsidized and highlighted theater of urban pomp and circumstance of the Hellenistic era and the Roman Empire.

The difference between the classical polis of the Athens model and the medieval city was, of course, self-rule. The classical Greek city governed itself, or believed it did so. The medieval city was the creature of a lord, a bishop, an abbott or some other feudal authority. The struggle for self-government began again in earnest only in the 12th century, rather late in the story. But when it did, when the commune began to rise against the feudal masters and demand charters of self-government, demolition came back as an instrument of the people. The classic example is late medieval Florence.

15th-century bird's-eye view of Florence

Detail of the plan of Rome showing the Via Giulia and the Banchi trident

Florence had been a perfect Roman city once, with a grid. It had been eaten into in the ways we described before. Thoroughfares, often whole neighborhoods, were obstructed and sealed off by feudal lords whose towers rose on the skyline of the city. Lesser infringements cluttered the city form everywhere, so the charge of the young republic beginning in the 12th century was two-pronged: to unstop urban passageways, weave together all quarters of the city and thus eradicate pockets of resistance against its authority; and, to conceive of the city form once again as an intentional design that confirmed the supremacy of the commune, the people and their institutions. Now the first of these objectives was of course achieved by legal constraint, by financial settlement, by the use of force. The government adopted a building code; statutes affecting the appearance and care of open spaces and public works were enforced so that everything was regulated, from balconies, porticoes and outer stairs, to street traffic and pavement. This was no mere aesthetic compunction. It was designed to allow no overwhelming private privileges such as feudal towers, that would create extravagant accents in the standard fabric. The height of feudal towers was systematically reduced. The property of offending nobles was razed. New public building was undertaken to make the prestige of the commune evident to itself and to the outside world.

The city as a work of art goes beyond mere practical amelioration, political control and the presumption of monumentality. It strives for what we might call perceivable order, that in turn relies on the ability to see the city as a ceremonial symbol. We have two direct indications that this trend existed in 13th-century Tuscany. First, we know of the drawing up of town plans, that was a way of conceiving of the city in its totality; and second, we know of the appointment of town architects. In 13th- and 14th-century Florence, an effort was made to combine the two great ideals of the Greco-Roman world—self-rule and the noble formalism of the Hellenistic planned city. So, for example, wide, straight streets again became a goal. The benefits of rectifying irregularities were said to be health, convenience and beauty,

words that you know we shall hear again and again from demolishers of all stripes in succeeding centuries. The details of Arnolfo di Cambio's Florentine master plan include a new cathedral and the palace of the people in the Piazza della Signoria. These were connected by a widened axis, the present Via Calzaioli, with Or San Michele, the city's granary and a monument to her guilds, halfway in-between. Perhaps the most important point: all of this was done in a participatory atmosphere. Artists as well as the people generally were active in this. Taxes and labor from the people went to the building of the new walls. Citizens' commissions oversaw street clearance and urban renewal projects. The guilds supervised construction of public buildings. There were competitions and juries, and the citizenry at large was, in fact, invited at times to testify on the projects. And the city form was coaxed into shape, with a little widening here and a little straightening out there.

That method continued in the Renaissance. Ideal schemes for perfect overall forms stayed in treatises. Reality forced a respect for built things as long as they were serviceable, as long as they could be kept standing. Urban stock was not casually expendable. So the new style had to rely on exemplary accent to make its point. Renaissance churches and palaces, prominently situated, would ennoble an old town. That is the story of Pienza, Mantua, Urbino.

But there were some important attitudinal changes. The destruction of contiguous tissue, of temporary accretions, in the name of morality and decorum, which had started with pre-Renaissance Florence, now becomes a common solution. And this works against the medieval notion I have discussed elsewhere, that large public structures must harbor humble attachments, that families of uses are more important than the purity of architectural forms. Then, with the Via Giulia in Rome, we have a very early example of a straight street that is run wilfully through a built area, running counter to the existing street net.

Aerial view of Rome showing the
Piazza Santa Maria della Pace

John Nash plan of project for Regents Park
and Street to St. James Park

Such behavior, however, was exceptional. In the Renaissance, cities changed primarily through individual negotiations between owners and builders on the one hand and the citizens' commissions responsible for streets on the other. The law begins to favor large dignified buildings in the new manner, and it provides that neighbors be obliged to sell adjacent property to those who propose to upgrade their building or to build a new one from the ground up. An owner could also barter privately for public land in order to adjust the shape of a block, to alter the alignment of neighboring facades, or even to change the width and direction of a street. That is the way—not through any great Renaissance master plan—that we get the great rectangular blocks of the Palazzo Farnese with its front piazza, and that is the way in which, through a matter of three centuries, the medieval fabric of the city of Rome, which was basically composed of two- or three-story single family dwellings, slowly begins to congeal, consolidate and enlarge itself into large apartment blocks. It was, in fact, this piecemeal way of changing the fabric of the city that was most crucial to the Renaissance and the Baroque rather than those great gestures that we like to talk about.

With the Baroque, and beginning with Michelangelo, of course, all those things that we associate with the Baroque come in: dynamism, impetuous reach, sensate passage through space and also a new notion of the grand vista. Renaissance streets, even when they are straight, like the Via Giulia, are essentially connecting channels of communication. They facilitate traffic and encourage the exploration of a quarter. But they are not conceived of as grand vistas with worthy termini. In Sixtus's famous scheme for Rome, he sends these impetuous avenues in all directions. You have bifocal framing of stretches of straight lines. You see out into something worthwhile at the end, an obelisk, an arch, or a monument of some kind, which is of course at the basis of so much of Napoleon's, Haussmann's and Mussolini's later planning.

In the hands of the unscrupulous, this kind of mentality could have meant disaster to old city fabrics. It didn't. As we said at the beginning, common practice was gentler and a lot more could be done with mock effects than downright destruction. The example of Baroque Rome is a wonderful case in point. To carve out a space in front of Santa Maria della Pace you don't demolish an entire area. You open a little piazza that will look enormous because of the narrow way you are going to be brought in, and you literally drop curtains that shield from the eye the irregularities that are behind. Another way that Rome is marvelous is in the way it takes areas that are a jumble in terms of open space and, by a single justified gesture—a fountain, or an obelisk—galvanizes and pulls together the space without doing anything to the edges. You can see what the gigantic, oversized fountain has done to the Piazza Barberini. Nothing is done around it; that fountain and its great jet are enough to pull the square together. This is in fact a new piazza, without actually having much new construction around it. A more famous case is the Piazza del Popolo of Rome where the idea of two small matching churches, like a triumphal arch of Christian intent at the end of the piazza leading to the city, is enough to transform this jumble of an ancient Roman gate, an obelisk and various kinds of buildings around it. The French model of the royal *place* with uniform facades and a single crown line on all sides, or for that matter the residential squares of London, unfold relatively harmlessly at the edges of town, and are therefore only of marginal interest in our context.

By 1750, the major changes that concern European urban structure are:
1. The cultural revolution, challenging the mid-18th century primacy of that classical language that had been ruling Europe since the early Renaissance. Archeological revivalism begins with an interest in all the past and its varied manifestations, introducing an emotional note into matters of urbanism. Slowly, very slowly, the notion is established that the fabric of a city with all the styles represented in it records the continuity of the race and that therefore planning cannot simply be content with motives of health, comfort and beauty. Memory as guiding principle of planning comes into play.

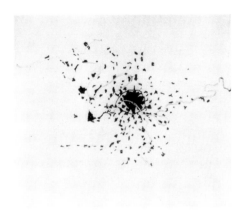

Plan of Paris   1850

Baron Haussmann's plan for the
Avenue de l'Opera, Paris

2. In association with revivalism is the notion of picturesqueness, in which various things stand together so that uniformity of design, and other tenets of Classicism will be brushed aside in things like Nash's Regent Street and Regents Park complex where a whole series of episodes exist together. Incident is worked into the scheme. Part of this picturesqueness is something done by Karl Friedrich Schinkel, who carefully sites single buildings in a way that recalls neighbors without forced parody. In this way, he seeks to unify an environment pictorially. Now, both the picturesque aesthetic of the Nash variety and Schinkelesque environmentalism make what exists acceptable and thus reduces the urge to demolish the old for the sake modern perfections.

3. These compromises with the ideal notions of classical design represent the decline of autocratic rule. The age of grandeur is now over. With the political and military revolutions of the end of the 18th century, we begin to come to grips with the triumph of capitalism and the bourgeoisie. This is one side of the change in the social order that preoccupies the 19th century. The other side is of course industrialism and its corollaries: swelling urban population, critical changes in transportation and the rise of a new class of professional administrators destined to cope with nightmarish problems of sanitation and general welfare. Both sides affect the old cores radically. The bourgeoisie wants now to reshape cities in its own image, to make its own businesses, residences and places of entertainment the monumental core of the city, replacing the princely palaces and royal churches of the Baroque period.

This is the triumph of Haussmann who is working for the Emperor to be sure, but a bourgeois Emperor, and the monied class that propped him up. This upper middle class of merchants, financiers and manufacturers, liberal in their business practices, but politically right-wing, demand law and order, favorable conditions for the conduct of their affairs, nice places to live and cultural and recreational centers for their leisure hours.

They want plumbing to work, they want the sewer mains to be in order, and these requirements Haussmann's *grands travaux* meet admirably. He reduces urban tensions and unrest by demolishing old neighborhoods that were chronic trouble spots. He rationalizes and streamlines the street network for rapid communication and weaves into it adequate business facilities. The mansard-roofed apartment houses that line his great boulevards provide gracious living for families no longer content with having an apartment in the side streets of the old parts of the city, but not rich enough to own townhouses of their own. But at the same time, in the execution of this remarkable feat, Haussmann proved himself the most able of the new breed of professional planners. Now, this group functions completely differently from the designers of late medieval Florence. And I think Haussmann himself feels that. In one point in his memoirs he makes a lengthy distinction between a commune and a prefecture. He says, "The commune is almost as old as the family; it is not simply a territorial division, it is a collection of people tied together by concerns at once moral and material. With us, [it has] become an integral and subordinate part of the State. . . . By contrast, the Department [of the Seine] . . . is above all an administrative division." Exactly so. It is a lot easier to see the city as plant, a design on paper you can update and modernize as needed, without having to worry about it as a collection of people for whom the city must struggle to maintain a moral and material fit.

Isn't this really the same argument we have today—the struggle between representative government, municipal bureaucrats on the one hand, and neighborhoods on the other? Aren't the aesthetics of demolition a polite cover for something far more basic? If what we look like in urban terms is what we are, who decides what we are going to look like is also deciding what we are, what we were, what we are going to be. Who is going to

View of a street in the medieval town of Rothenburg, on the Tauber River, West Germany

do this? Will it be the ruler? Will it be the people? The civic government? Now one side of the argument is the choice between the total power and action of central authority (Haussmann with the aid of Napoleon III), and the piecemeal compromising urbanism of representative government. But there is another side of the argument: whether you see the city as a collection of people, of generations, fixed to the place with conviction, proud of its past, aware of its traditions, solicitous of its future; or the city as an amenity where people live and work as it suits their convenience, where their commitment is conditional and short-term. In both these contexts demolition is not a simple matter of health, economics, traffic, beauty; it is a statement of purpose, made by a society to itself and to those who will view it in the future.

Now, the 19th century was really very confused about that. The cities were changing fast, alarmingly fast. The development of the periphery dissipated the traditional energies of the city, confused its identity. The Baroque city, however explosive within, was a closed city. The new Vienna, the new Paris, were not. In the past, the city had been the rock of existence for those who lived there. It was the familiar slowly changing backdrop of the evolving generations, the material covenant of spelled-out relationships. You were born in it to stay, you knew it well, it had palpable shapes and it commanded deep allegiance. Now the city behaved erratically. It showed a protean impatience beyond the common will. Waves of immigrants jostled it rudely; it pushed out messily, shapelessly, it was too big to comprehend, except on paper. Charles Baudelaire said it best and most simply of the changes Haussmann had wrought for Paris: "The old Paris," he said, "is no more. The city's form, alas, changes faster than the human heart."

One reaction was to cling to what was there. Urban conservation. It is a minority view slow to mature, gaining real strength only toward the end of the century. And even then the initial fight was for monuments, buildings of artistic or historic interest. Haussmann challenges his detractors in his memoirs to show "even a single old monument worthy of interest, one building precious for its art, curious

by its memories," which his administration destroyed. He doesn't see the irony because he has a very special meaning of what *worthy* tissue is. He doesn't see the irony in the list of 19,722 houses destroyed by him in greater Paris, of which 4,300-odd were in the old core. It is okay because they were worthless, unhealthy. He says he supplied 43,000 new houses or repaired old ones, so what is the fuss? People can move and live somewhere else.

Painfully, slowly the awareness of contexts dawns, and that primarily in Germany, where the concept of *Stadtbild,* or the general physiognomy of a place as a monument finds expression. The city and its landscape, its identity, its character, after the war of 1870, became a concern in Germany. The patriotic movement called Heimatschutz began to equate conservation with nationalism. Now some really remarkable prescriptions come out of Bavarian and Hessian law around 1900, and local building regulations of towns like Hildesheim. "In the streets and open places . . . those parts of any building which can be seen from any street or public place must be carried out in architectural forms that agree with those previously in use in Germany up to the middle of the 17th century. Further, the new work must as far as possible be in harmony with its nearest surroundings and especially with any conspicuous building that gives character to a whole neighborhood. As a rule, new buildings must be built so that the general appearance of the surroundings is not interfered with. This applies especially to materials, including those used in the roofing and the ornamentation, and to coloring."

The nationalistic argument strengthened the hand of the aesthetic theories persuasively put forth by Sitte, Stübben, Brinckmann and others—that straight, wide avenues can be boring and vacuous; that the small incident, the twisted street, the rounded corner, the little planted oasis unexpectedly come upon were superior to mansarded boulevards, *rond-points* and imposing *places.* This helped to stem for a while the process of the Haussmannization of European cities. It made it aesthetically chic to tolerate the clutter of old cities, to change them gently, lovingly. Thus, Rome could produce Corso Vittorio Emanuele, gingerly threading its way among important buildings.

But what the Heimatschutz crowd was getting at was something beyond mere theory of form, beyond the selective memory of monuments. The burgomeister of Hildesheim, in a speech to a conference on the care of monuments held in Düsseldorf in 1902, gave the classic defense of this point of view:

Does a civic administration exist merely for the sake of enabling people to fulfill the needs of daily life as well, as cheaply and as completely as possible? Is the city there for this alone? . . . Does the well-being of men consist only in bodily things, or is there not something far higher, the spiritual well-being of men, and does it not contribute greatly to this when they feel in close relation to the past, and take delight in realizing how the city has gradually built itself up, and how not only the streets, but every single public building, each individual house, even each piece of carved ornament, has grown in the course of time to be what it is? To make this feeling real is the task of the civic authorities.

But to accomplish this task civic authorities need, first, to curb the profit machine, the new all-consuming speculative greed. Many cities can't or don't. Florence, once a model of civic mettle, lost its historic downtown to speculation. It substituted a grid that was supposed to bring back the Roman grid and didn't; and it acquired a most authentic looking Renaissance downtown, almost all of it ersatz 1880s stuff totally without authenticity, standing on an area of 70,000 square meters that was wiped clean of 26 old streets, 20 piazzas, 341 houses and 451 shops.

Second, to achieve the burgomeister's task civic authorities are needed who are elected and accountable to the people, not appointed and ultimately responsible to the state. The commune that Haussmann was glad to be rid of or the representative apparatus of civic administration that Mussolini—and his proclaimed archetype, Augustus—abolished, as soon as possible, are essential. With this elective body out

of the way the stage is set for the regime to remember selected great deeds suitable for the glorification of its own aims. Then, in the name of saving monuments, of decorum, health, *grandezza,* the regime will attack the most defenseless unresisting bits of city, the live tissue around the solid anchors of historic piles, the tissue that happens unfailingly to be the densest and most restive neighborhoods of working-class families, the urban poor, small craftspeople or *artigiani.* In the process the regime manages to eradicate an unwanted, volatile social element from the hearts of cities, the one most likely to become antagonistic to or disillusioned with the regime.

The hate of totalitarian rule for incidental form is understandable. The urban clutter that fascists disparagingly called local color is the sum total of small idiosyncracies, hundreds of semi-witting acts of taking possession of a city. It is eloquent of the continuous rhythms of a common humanity that survives regimes, digests extravagant triumphs and defeats, that goes on weaving a pattern of personal joy and pain and decency. It is incompatible with what the fascists called *gerarchia,* where individualism did not exist outside of the place to which each person was assigned in society according to his or her function in a chain of authority that culminated with the Duce. Fascist *sventramenti* are bothersome because they remind us of a people's long acquiescence. Similar totalitarian schemes should bother us today, whatever their source: dictators, spineless city councils that cannot stand up to private interests, form-givers like Le Corbusier.

Contextualism is not a war won. It is never won with finality. The city-form always demands vigilance. Not to be bothered by the loss of past buildings, big and small, is to have no sense of community beyond our immediate needs and pleasures. To feel that loss, to resist it, is to remember the times when all too spinelessly we surrendered our destiny to high designs, and to refuse to allow it to happen again. To kill is not to heal. To destroy is never a wise way to foster love.

Building Club Sandwiches

Charles Moore
with Urban Innovations Group and
Ron Filson, August Perez, Malcolm Heard,
Allen Eskew and Christine Beebe
Piazza d'Italia Fountain
New Orleans, Louisiana   1977–78

● *Charles Moore*

Architects, I believe, come in two groups. One group sets up a theory, a framework of what it thinks is right and important and then either writes or talks or draws or, in some increasingly rare cases these days, makes buildings that demonstrate its theories. There are others of us who have some chemical compulsion to make buildings and we invent theories to describe why those are the right buildings to have made and why some other kind of building would have been totally inappropriate or irrelevant. I make no bones about belonging to the second group.

Over the last couple of decades I've thought of various ways to describe, to make theories or metaphors about those things that seem to me very important. It's not like making proposals in more readily provable scientific fields. It does seem to me possible, however, to phrase reasons why some things are pleasurable to many of us and why other things, mostly of more recent times, are less pleasurable and need to be superseded by something else.

Buildings are recipients of human energy, care and love and if they get enough of it, they, like the biblical parable of bread cast upon the water, come back club sandwiches; they pay back to us what we have put into them. Having gathered our energies, they give us back pleasure in the sense that dancers call being centered. It is the sense that we are somewhere in someplace and that it's ours and that we belong on the face of this planet in just the spot where we are. In order for buildings to be loved, to be the center of energy, they have to get energy not only from the architects and the contractors who build them, but especially from the inhabitants and maybe even from the people who are paying for them. They have to soak it up from everybody involved.

If we could look among the many things that seem to have gone wrong with the building of buildings and cities in our own time, the one that seems to me the most important is that we architects have made of designing buildings an act so exclusive and elitist after the 1960s that they simply aren't getting energy from the people who use them. Instead, these people are complaining about how they can't find the front door, or how their flat roofs leak. So it seems to me that what we have to do to make buildings that give people the feeling that they are in the center of the world, is to make buildings that can absorb the care and energy of most everybody. And to an increasing extent, that seems to mean buildings that the inhabitants feel they have designed.

I don't know how many architectural conventions I've attended where I've been told that the most important thing on the agenda was to educate the public. That meant, I gathered, to brainwash the public into believing that what we were providing was the right thing instead of questioning it too closely. To tell them, when they started complaining about not being able to find the front door, that if they were only properly educated they wouldn't care whether they found the front door or not.

makes some architectural elements for the front door, most particularly a pair of columns that flank it. These are lovingly invested with energy, made special with his time and care. The columns become vertical stand-ins for the parents and the love they bear their children.

A quite different scene, but still with some of the same stuff, comes in south German Baroque churches where columns stand free and special, where they start rather above your head, so that you're in a position of separation from them. They represent humankind but humankind soaring up into the vault of heaven where all those angels are carrying on. In France's St. Trophime at Arles, the arch, the entablature, the columns holding it up, the gabled roof, are all part of an age-old way of building things. That automatically means something to the people who come there, as C.G. Jung spent a lot of time explaining. Ordinary buildings have those same elements.

Signs are very much discussed these days but they've been there all the while with their special sentiments added to the basic shapes of buildings. The bronze doors of St. Zeno in Verona have been in place for 700 years to describe the biblical stories familiar to people who go through them. The Santo Domingo trading post in New Mexico gives us information that's a little bit less traditional but not unexpected. We've been taught that cosmetic concerns are not supposed to be of interest to us. But in the same way that people have described their desire to have us relate to them by putting cosmetics on their faces, so buildings, given the existence of paint, have the capacity to endear themselves to us through their surfaces, whether it's paint, as in a house in Dolores Hidalgo, or pieces of corn, as in the Corn Palace in Mitchell, South Dakota, which as you know is changed every little while when the corn starts to fall off. The very act of renewing it, as in Japan, where the great Shinto Shrines of Ise are rebuilt every 20 years as an act of caring again, of making things new though continuous, seem to me well embodied in this exciting piece of history in South Dakota.

That was so even a decade ago. Now it seems to me that at the same conventions I'm hearing people talk about the importance of learning from people. Not of brainwashing, but of finding out what really matters to them and trying to deal with that. A book by Bill Hubbard called *Complicity and Conviction Towards an Architecture of Convention,* in spite of its post-Venturi title is, it seems to me, a very important piece of work. In it the author provides a set of very persuasive parallels between architecture and law. He makes the point that in Anglo-Saxon law, judges make decisions that change greatly over the decades and the centuries, depending on the spirit of the times and what the people of the times think is right. They never just dump all the decisions that have been made before. They make new decisions accepting all those that have been made before and adding some appropriate new ingredients that leave all of the old ones intact but make a new decision more correct. Architects in our century, since 1910 or 1915, have been so busy announcing that everything that people are used to and that has gone before is junk and needs to be superseded by some revolutionary new shape, that in addition

to running out of revolutionary new shapes, we've pretty well lost the public, the people who might feel comfortable with what they're getting. I'm fond of noting that what architects do is make a kind of choreography of the familiar. And then the surprising has to be there to wake up people and even to make the familiar recognizable.

It's important to note that human constructions through all of civilization have been celebrations of ourselves and especially of the characteristic unique among creatures on this planet, shared only in fact by penguins—that we stand up. Consequently, verticality means a great deal to humankind. It's interesting that when humans build a cathedral, they tend to build it high, in some kind of celebration of themselves. Those columns that we've made through our history have an enormous power to say things to us and to receive our love and care and attention. I'm particularly fond of the houses in the Mexican state of Michoacan that are one- or two-room log cabins. They are built by the parents of a young couple about to be married. After the marriage, the parents load them onto a cart and take them to set up housekeeping in another place. The father of the bride or groom, by tradition,

House in Michoacan, Mexico, showing columns made by the parents of a newly married couple

Santo Domingo Trading Post
New Mexico

Corn Palace
Mitchell, South Dakota

One of the things about us as Americans is that we're not a nation of unpretentious peasants connected to the land, throbbing to the rhythms of the soil. We are in fact invaders, and rather pretentious ones. My great grandfather, for example, who was a farmer in Michigan, kept his farm logs in Latin and his personal diaries in Greek and lived in a Greek revival farm house, a very beautiful one that's still there. He grew perfectly good corn in perfectly good fields in southern Michigan, and he had as part of him not only that but also the classical past. I think all of us in our various ways and with our various emphases are part not only of where we happen to be but also of a continuing Western tradition, some part or another of which is likely to interest us very much. There are connections with the natural world that come in many places and in various walks of life. A cottage at Balmoral, one of the British royal family's Scottish retreats, is full of the same combination of uprightness and attempts to be natural as a little cemetery in a not very rich part of Cuernavaca, Mexico. And people maintain ancient traditions in the shapes they learn and choose. The experience of sitting, just being somewhere, has been made a lot of in all kinds of places across the planet. The towns in the north of Spain where sunshine is very much prized sport a kind of bay window outside the doors that keeps the cold out, into which people can go to soak up the sun.

The relation in size of us to where we are is a marvelously variable and manipulable relationship. In Thomas Jefferson's house at Monticello, it is said he invented the triple-hung window. The bottom two of three panels in a long window slide up to cover the top panel and leave a space something over six-feet high for people to walk through, as in a door. You become little if you go through a great big window, at least littler than you expect to be. The opposite occurs in Daitoku-ji in Kyoto, a Buddhist temple where even for short 17th-century Japanese people, the railing around the walkway was very low. You find yourself in a place overlooking a garden, all of which is miniature. You soar above it as a creature at once there and not there, too big for it, watching a magical, reduced, miniaturized world. Again, the big and little are manipulated over and over.

Thomas Jefferson, when he designed his university, had in mind that architecture would serve to advertise his brand new and not very rich country to the whole world by using the shapes of the Greek and Roman Republics to make the right thing for the new American Republic. With his ten pavilions for professors and the students' rooms colonnaded in front of, or behind or past them, he made a fully orchestrated demonstration of some kind of connivance between the aristocratic pretensions of the pavilions and the democratic insistence of the student colonnaded chambers.

One of my favorite buildings, now gone, was a church in Croten Falls, New York, with unmatched towers, like Chartres Cathedral. Its builders in the late 19th century clearly had seen at least postcards of Chartres, and they wanted to make their own thing that made a connection with the then 700-year-old building, that didn't try to leave it behind but rather continued it. They didn't have stone, they were carpenters and they had wood. So they made with the wood, turned and jigsawed in the highest technical ways available to them, twin porches, and amazing moldings and lacy, beautiful towers. At once they were continuing a tradition and starting something new made with their own hands and care.

Charles Moore and William Turnbull
Kresge College
University of California at Santa Cruz   1972

In discussing building projects from my office I've selected five that represent how far we knew how to go with the support and involvement of other people than ourselves, usually the client. First a college, the campus of the University of California at Santa Cruz. It is in a redwood forest that should have been a national park and not a campus. It is very beautiful and has three meadows. We were involved with the campus planning and with one of the residential colleges. Ours was the sixth college conceived by the chancellor of the campus. He had gone to Williams College in Massachusetts when it had 600 students, and he felt, tradition being tradition, that 600 was the right size for a college to be. The chancellor was interested in making a new campus that was, they thought then, to hold 27,500 students, like all the campuses in the 1960s. So he was going to make a bunch of 600-student colleges, a system that has just this year been finally wiped out. They'd had five and we were the sixth. We did the planning that told us pretty firmly where the college ought to be located. Rather than siting it on the border line between the meadows and the redwood forest, we located it in the redwood forest itself where there are some fairly bare places.

We were ten years in planning the college. We put classrooms in the middle of the street with parking underneath so that the cars would be out of the way. The classrooms have sod roofs so that when you look out of your window, instead of seeing across into the windows opposite, you see sheep safely grazing on the sod roofs. And we made special places like a monumental snack bar in the center and worked on schemes for a variety of living spaces that didn't seem like the standard

dormitory rooms along an endless corridor. In 1964 when we started, males and females were still separated in colleges, and this was an attempt to have ground floor living rooms shared by both sexes. Then a middle floor of bedrooms—bed/study/sitting rooms—very flexible, 8 feet by 8 feet that were divisible in many ways. On the top floor, men's and women's places for baths, for sunbathing and informal television watching and not-many-clothes segregated places. By the time we had been through three governorships, the budget had been cut I don't remember how many times, and mores had changed too, so the final version was much cheaper and more suitable to the times. It was a set of four-person, double bedroom apartments, that turns out to be the least expensive thing you can make and much more prized. In the process, over the ten years, from the early 60s to the early 70s, we'd made it inexpensive enough to be directly competitive with the schlock two-story stud and stucco apartments that builders/developers were making around the campus and making it as loose and informal as those places. By this time the college was very liberal in its views, and had a student committee that was telling us what it wanted. We didn't know quite how to handle the committee and got into trouble more than once. For example, the college is named Kresge because the University received support from the Kresge Foundation. After serious scholarship, we found the last old beautiful Kresge dime store sign in Detroit and we managed to acquire it and bring it west to put over the entrance. Well, the students announced that that was commercial and they were into woodburning, and so they made a sign. That's participation as it started for us.

We did lots of things with paint that we thought were important. The backs of all the arcades are bright colored from red through red-orange to orange to yellow-orange to yellow between the bottom and the top of the street. In special places they are painted special bright colors or patterns. We discovered it was best to paint at Christmas time when all the students had gone away because getting agreement on the color of paint for anything turned out to be past our capacity then or now. We did paint the side that faced the street two shades of white and the side that faces the forest a kind of ochre color, and then painted what we thought were special things like the door frames and railings blue. The students were very intent on not even naming the important public rooms because in the best Judeo-Christian tradition they said names are very important and it was not our province to give those names. They would find their own names. So we did persuade them to let us put numbers on the students' rooms, but the main spaces were left alone. A couple of years later I did notice they had acquired names, not very surprising names, library for library, common room for the common room, and so forth.

We decided our best bet was to make a great point of the trivial monuments. Things like telephone booths that people couldn't possibly feel any Judeo-Christian proprietary qualities about. The laundromat was one of the places that they had no special feelings about and so we painted it the brightest yellow we could find and asserted ourselves. I had a powerful desire to have the speaker's rostrum look like Abraham Lincoln's second inaugural platform, but at that time for some reason the University put its foot down and said that was a communist concept and so it ended up with simple stripes. I was pleased that the rostrum was on top of the garbage bin.

A decade later, a competition for a design for the Piazza d'Italia was being sponsored by the Italian community in New Orleans. It was a six-way competition and we were second prize winners. We didn't win the prize but some very good people in the office of August Perez did win it and we became the fountain consultants. We started by designing the fountain in the shape of Italy; and then we decided that water should run through the Po, Arno and Tiber rivers. As most people in New Orleans of Italian descent are Sicilian descent, it was clear that Sicily should be the center of this map, and in fact it became a speakers rostrum from which you can talk; you can sit on Sardinia and listen. All of this was worked out with very close connections with the Italian community that was sponsoring. We argued that we didn't have enough water for a real fountain. This was going to be a real bang up fountain and needed lots of water splashing. And so, what else was Italian? Well, I think it was I who announced that the classical orders of architecture were Italian with a little help from the Greeks, and that we might have all five of them, but with water squirting out. So we tried to invent various ways of using the Greek orders. We made a lot of studies in which we attempted to make acanthus leaves as would befit a composite column capital, and to make an egg and dart motif out of water squirting into spoons that might then go into an entablature. There are now lots of Italian festivals in the place and eventually there will be shops and restaurants around the Piazza to give the area daily as well as holiday life.

Charles Moore
with Moore Grover Harper,
Lorenz and Williams and J.P.C. Floyd
Riverdesign Dayton
Dayton, Ohio 1975

Dayton, Ohio, had a terrible flood in 1913 that killed a lot of people, and so they put up a high set of banks that pretty much hid the river from the city. Recently, there has been a lot of controversy about doing something to make the river pretty. The Miami flows right through the downtown and they are building a new low level bridge, a low level dam and making the river, finally, usable for recreation. The local bicycle company had helped sponsor a bicycle path along the river, but the inner city neighborhoods that share the waterfront were suspicious of others doing something that they weren't informed about and didn't agree with. So we went for the job in competition with several experienced firms. We had to figure out some new means to get close to a large number of people. So it came over us all of a sudden that television is a medium not much used by architects to make contact with people. And so our proposal included executive committees—a committee of 50 from the inner city neighborhoods represented, to participate in workshops, to say what they wanted and how they wanted it. Our proposal included six one-hour television programs on the local public station, staged about a month apart, with six telephone lines staffed by volunteers, so people could call in during the program and say what they wanted. We all sat and acted like architectural short-order cooks drawing up whatever anybody called in. We thought we'd have some trouble with that, but it turned out to our astonishment and delight that there were almost no conflicts that couldn't be handled by simple, geographical means. Conflicting uses were kept away from each other. The ideas that people called in were almost all useful, thoughtful and largely doable. I remember making a major gaff: a man called asking where the UFO landing place was and I laughed. I could have told him there were 50 of them, but I was young then.

Our first step was to invite people who were interested in the city for a walk along the river, that many of them had never looked at, and for picnic lunches on the levy with gypsy violinists and other entertainment. People sketched and made records of what they saw and what they thought according to a rather elaborate program we had made up. We had a storefront office where some 2,000 people dropped in and told us what they were interested in. We did everything from serious discussions with local leaders to role playing in which we asked people to pretend that they were various persons going by the river and asking them what they would like to see there. Then we went on television six times. Chad Floyd, my partner, organized things so that people understood what we were talking about in this largely unfamiliar territory. We made models, simple block models, that showed the things that they and we had talked about for a six-acre downtown site that was prime real estate. People could call up and say, "Get that high rise right out of there, I hate it!" and we'd pick it up and yank it out. And then somebody else would call and say, "You put that high rise right back, that's where I want to be." And we then made a final presentation model, which we went through carefully with the high rise back in, and with condominiums along the river bank. With the Kiwanis Club and a garden club, we made a fountain to go out in the river. There's some mid-range stuff that's been built but the long-range plans haven't happened yet.

We were smarter by the time we did the second town plan in Roanoke, Virginia. There we worked with a CBS station and only four programs beautifully put together by the CBS people and ourselves. For the first time in ten years, we managed to get a whole set of bond issues passed to do things that people wanted.

One of the really critical things about all this, I think, is that if we the architects enter with a hidden agenda, we've had it. That is, if we want a set of things and we let that show even a little bit, kiss them good-bye. If, however, we drift in with an open mind and an avuncular smile and the desire to have people have what they care about, then the chances for getting it are very good.

We've done a couple of plans without television that seem to be working. Both are in California, where a local group in a workshop produces the design. The first is a park in the little town of Seal Beach in Orange County just below Los Angeles, where there was a lot of quite bitter conflict about whether an eight-acre site that belongs to the Los Angeles Department of Water and Power should be bought as a public park; what combination of public and private ownership would make it economically possible and still basically an open space for the people in the town who wanted it very much? Jim Burns of Halprin, Burns "take-part workshops" fame and we set up a workshop to see what people wanted. We put up big signs and had four evening workshops, a month apart, in which people could come and design it themselves. The first one was an awareness walk, as we've come to call them, where people got familiar with and wrote down observations in notebooks, made sketches, got to feel comfortable with the place. Then they came back, drew their notions on the floor on a roll of paper, wrote down things that mattered to them and with sixth grade kid parts—including fruit loops, a basic design tool for these purposes, as well as cellophane—made schemes for the park. This exercise produced a model with a whole bunch of interchangeable parts and lots of people arguing for various arrangements. It had a complicated set of economic parameters and we didn't want to talk in terms of dollars as that causes old-timers to say, "I can remember, sonny, when that much money would have bought the whole state of California."

Charles Moore
with Moore Ruble Yudell
St. Matthew's Episcopal Church
Pacific Palisades, California
now under construction

The last of these projects is a church in Pacific Palisades, a wealthy western suburb of Los Angeles, near Malibu, with an Episcopal parish that had had a long conflict over the selection of a new rector, after its rector of some 30 years had retired. They perceived themselves as not being able to agree about what day it was and so they wrote into the contract with their architects (and they interviewed a great number) that to build a new church, needed because their old one had burned in a forest fire, the architects would have to get a 67-percent vote of agreement by the parish for whatever scheme and location they came up with. We thought it was an interesting task and again called on Jim Burns to help us because we couldn't imagine that anything that we or anybody else would design could get that kind of support in those circumstances. The only possibility was for the parish to design it themselves with us helping. So we bought the fruit loops and the cellophane and had awareness walks. People made quite beautiful churches. And many serious discussions took place on how things should relate to each other. There were four all-day Sunday sessions. There were usually about 150 parishioners who took part in these out of a parish of about 350. We discovered that when we really pushed something, we lost it. The magic moment occurred at the end of the second workshop when the participants all had the same plan. They wanted to get as close to the altar as they could. They didn't want to go so far around it that they were looking at each other, so they wanted about a half-circle or ellipse of seating. By the end of that workshop we had the plan. We also made a kind of Rorschach test of slides, all mixed up, with two questions to be written down for each of 80 slides. One, do you like this? And two, would you like this for St. Matthew's? It turned out that although they all kept saying they wanted a dark wood church (the other church had been that), the three slides of a white church by Alvar Aalto, consistently were the leading vote getters. The church that received the fewest votes, or the most negative votes, "We do not want this for St. Matthew's," was St. Peter's in Rome! So we at least knew something about what they did not want.

The third workshop involved our coming with a set of building shapes—in model form—that would cover the planned shapes that they had come up with. The parishioners were asked to consider those and make whatever combination of plan and enclosure that appealed to them. They came with drawings; they gave us rather strong orders. More glass to the ground. The rector was opposing this one since he didn't want to be in competition with the squirrels outside, but the feeling was very strong and he did some compromising. But again there was almost complete agreement on what they wanted it to look like as well as what they wanted . . . how they wanted it to function in plan. So we drew the results of their desires with a half elliptical seating arrangement under a Latin cross roof with a bell wall which has since turned into a tower, with lots of glass to the ground and a very simple interior.

It's at once a simple chapel and a church with a rose window in it. It gives out double signals. We made a model and left it for a month for people to consider. They proposed some slight changes and we got an 83-percent vote of the parish who had designed it in favor of the scheme that they had designed.

Dayton and Roanoke, and Seal Beach, and especially St. Matthew's are, then, designs in which others, often many others, have had a strong hand. And I'm often asked, especially by architects if I, trained to give shape to things, don't feel disappointed and unfulfilled when the shape is fixed by so many other people. To which the answer, of course, is no: there is a great deal for the serious architect to do, focusing the vision of others, perfecting the shape of something they know they want, rather than something the architect has persuaded them they should have. "God," Mies van der Rohe noted, "is in the details," and that is where the experienced professional really gets to do his stuff, to tune fine a scheme that already means a great deal to people who feel the pride of ownership, of having created a place full blown. In the 60s, young and enthusiastic architects and planners thought that "advocacy planning" would let people produce the schemes that somehow lay perfect in their heads, so they might perform like midwives, might be ready to help pop whatever kind of Minerva out of the head of Zeus. Mostly it didn't work, the ideas weren't fully enough formed to be born. It became apparent that there are critical acts for the architect to perform: to encourage people's dreams and images into existence; to shape them so that their original creators will view them with pride, will continue to invest them with their energy and care, and will reap the continuing rewards that buildings full of human energy repay.

Setting the Stage for Human Encounter

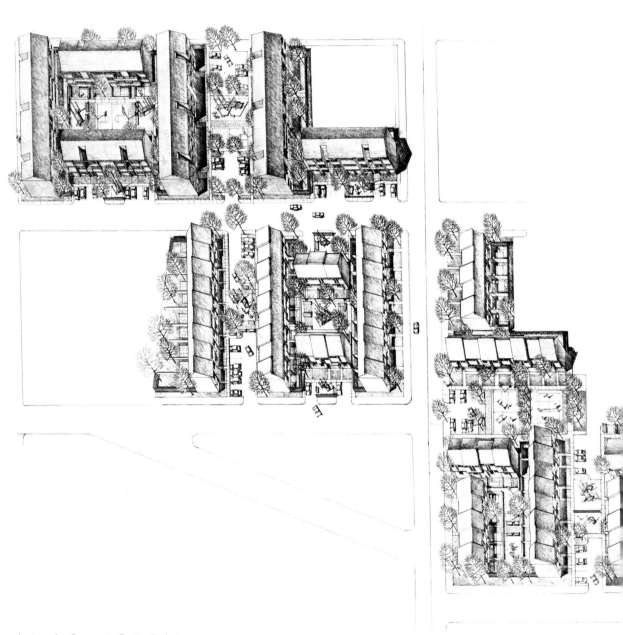

Institute for Community Design Analysis
Moderate-income housing for the city of
Newark, New Jersey
Aerial view of the proposed four-block
development showing three-story walk-ups
and a high-rise building for the elderly
in the lower right.

Oscar Newman

For most of the history of civilization the major concern of architects was the clothing of buildings in skins that would evoke proper astonishment and veneration. Architects, as we have come to know those who designed the monuments of history (from the Egyptian tombs to the palaces of the Renaissance) had the job of fashioning the houses of power: citadels for the wealthy, for the church and for the state. Little attention was paid to the utility of the spaces enclosed within these awe-inspiring buildings; it didn't have to be. The activities housed were comparatively simple, and there was always more room available than was really needed. The entry halls, corridors and stairwells of many of these buildings take up more space than the rooms they lead to. One could learn to make do.

With the coming of the Industrial Revolution and the urbanization of society, permanent buildings were constructed to house the activities not only of the powerful but of everyone in society: factories overwhelmed churches and palaces in their size and complexity; permanent housing for the working and middle classes took up 90 percent of the land area of cities. But just as wealth began to be more evenly distributed, so was the range of activities given permanent enclosure. Competition for enclosed space in the urban setting became severe; every square inch began to count. It was no longer possible to be concerned simply with fashioning monumental or pictorial facades; the utility of the inside space became equally important. A quiet but insistent revolution took place in the

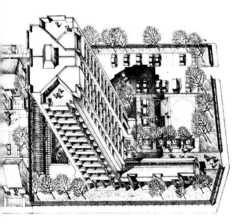

method of designing buildings: the internal functions became too complex to be strait-jacketed into the predetermined forms of a single historical style; now they dictated the forms of building exteriors. Much of the reason for the success of the eclectic style that flourished for over a century prior to modernism, is that it provided a language of forms that could encompass complex, open-ended spatial programs.

With the Industrial Revolution, architects who had hitherto been content to serve only the select and the powerful, began to feel the need to serve a cross section of society. But the design of factories and workers' housing projects was not initially the accepted province of architects: these buildings were designed either by engineers or by developers. Nevertheless, even with the commitment to a new clientele, the old habits were found to die hard. The newly committed architect who began designing for the limited resources of the mass society had been educated in the same tradition as those who designed for the comparatively unlimited wealth of the chosen few. The results were, as a consequence, not always satisfactory. Minimal workers' apartments were squeezed into edifying neoclassical facades—a far less successful product than the endless, engineer-designed row houses that surrounded factories throughout England.

Brinkmann and Van der Flugt
Van Nelle tobacco factory
Rotterdam   1928
In its provisions for natural light and air,
recreation rooms and dining facilities,
this building compares well with the best
contemporary working environments.

There was a time not that many years ago—and in retrospect what a glorious and inspiring time it was—when modern buildings were actually designed from inside out, when architects began their designs by first considering the people and activities to be housed. That was during the 1920s and 1930s—the pioneering period of the modern movement—and nothing we have built since has equaled the revolutionary spirit and unfettered imagination evident in those buildings. They heralded the common man and his daily pursuits. They were built minimally but well. Their luxury lay in the quantities of space and light provided, not in the materials, the detailing, the skillfully fashioned facades. But it did not take too long for that revolutionary spirit to become subverted, its goals and commitments forsaken. Bald-faced and innocent of thought, architects returned to their old ways with the inevitability of addicts hooked on accustomed highs. Using the new ingredients (or form language) of modernism, they embarked upon the grand road of a new style: the modern "style" replaced the grab bag of historical eclecticism. Exposed steel I-sections became a substitute for fluted Doric columns; plate glass supplanted polished granite facades. Buildings stopped being designed from inside out and began being designed, in the modern idiom, from outside in. And what happened to the form generating role of the internal activities? As a design methodology it was abandoned. The important lessons learned in the pioneering period of the 20s and 30s were forgotten in the undertow of World War II. In the post-World War II period we were brought to the ultimate irony: modern, functional looking buildings that didn't work. They were not only dysfunctional, they often proved totally uninhabitable.

Something else was learned during that pioneering period, something even more important than that the governing form of a building is to be generated by its internal activities. Although I am an advocate of functionalism, I'm not sure I am a devout believer. It is something else that I believe in, and that something else is the subject of this essay: the spaces provided by an architect can lead people to doing new things, to thinking about themselves in different ways, and to engaging in activities with others that they would not have contemplated if these spaces were not provided. It is a small conceptual step beyond functionalism, but it is critical—so critical a departure from previous architectural pursuits as to change the entire role of the profession—at least in my view.

It is the specter of determinism that is being raised here—the specter that haunted social science for almost a century. How dare one even think, let alone say, that the shape of spaces provided by an architect could lead people into activities and associations with others that a lack of such spaces would negate? It is social-science sacrilege to say that the human animal might be led by his physical environment to perform new tricks. Thinking man is not supposed to do that; he is supposed to have a will of his own and predetermined goals and is supposed to be able to carry them out, space willing or not. Well, we'll see. I'm as much the believer in the thinking, free-willed man as the next person, but I must say, I don't think the beast lurks very far behind.

There are obvious limits to the ways in which space can be manipulated to affect people's behavior: people will not be led to doing what they don't want to do, only into adopting behavior that is self-fulfilling. But even such selfish behavior can have socially beneficial side effects. To understand how people can be led to doing things unconsciously, one must first begin with the careful study of how people use and differentiate their existing environments. In examining housing (the same attitudes apply to schools, office buildings or shops), we will begin by trying to make simple but important differentiations and move on to how the designer can manipulate these differences. I will be discussing two elements of design in housing: the design of physical space, and the design for social groupings—both the province of the architect-planner.

54

One of the things that brought the flood of immigrants to America in the mid-19th and early-20th centuries was their desire to own their own homes. In photographs taken from the 1860s to the early 1900s people are seen landing in America in sailboats and steamships, proudly standing next to kegs of nails, because in America they intended to build themselves a house. They were obsessed with a vision of their own home on its own piece of land. It might be small, it might be stark, it might not have much light, but it would belong to them and only to them. They could control the space within it and the ground immediately around it. And even when the primitive log cabin was transferred to a setting which was more urban, you still found that much concern was given to defining the individual house on its separate piece of land. But as our cities became areas of still greater opportunity and as the rural and small-town populations flooded into them, we reached the point where siting each unit on its own piece of land became impossible. The dictates of density challenged this most fundamental of American dreams.

This concentration of population in cities was of course occurring in all industrializing countries. Unfortunately the solutions worked out for creating more dense human habitations in urban settings did not start with the premise: how do we capture the environment of the single-family house in a multi-family situation, but rather began with the abandonment of the single-family house concept and the search for a new one. Thus the Swiss-French architect Le Corbusier, faced with the problem of high density design, would not lower himself to examining how the existing five and six story apartment walk-ups of Paris succeeded in capturing the look and feel of the single-family house, but instead embarked upon a new vision—one that allowed him to feed his stylistic inclinations.

Le Corbusier disparaged the notion of the single-family house on its own piece of land and ridiculed the idea of hearth and home. He called the industrial city built of dense concentrations of single-family houses ludicrous. Unité Habitation in Marseilles is a utopian vision of a new society—a communal society in which individual grounds or lots are done away with. Le Corbusier's unsupported notions were adopted in America after World War II in the construction of many public housing projects. In St. Louis, Minoru Yamasaki, working with a density that would have allowed high rises or three-story walk-ups, chose the high rise solution. He used Le Corbusier's Marseilles flats as his model. In his plan the grounds were to be free of buildings and individual lots. The apartment buildings were to stand above the ground, and a river of trees (as the architect called it) would flow between the buildings. And it was an interesting notion, it was a utopian notion, and utopias have their place: they help to give focus to our dreams and provide a new mystique, a new religion we can follow. The problem with building utopias or generating utopias that are not based on a very careful examination of what people want or what people do or how people live, is that these utopias are false and when we build them we pay a terrible price. Here, the counterpart of freeing the ground was to make streets in the air. The idea was that if you put enough people up in the air they would get together on those streets. Again it was a notion that was not born of any particular experience but was rather hypothetical, growing totally out of the architect's mind. When the environment was built, the ground down below was not really a river of trees and the apartments were not really all that desirable. The streets in the air didn't really work. The play areas down below were so distant from the home that mothers could not allow their children to go there. The interior environment they had to move through was too anonymous, too frightening, both within the building and without. And the project never filled up fully. The streets in the air, those lovely places where children were to play and mothers do their wash, became huge garbage pits.

Minoru Yamasaki
Model for Pruitt-Igoe housing project
St. Louis, Missouri 1955

Pruitt-Igoe's "streets in the air," disreputable in their final days before demolition.

Somehow, in looking for the solution to high density residential environments we have come too far away from our original obsession with the individual family house on its own piece of land. Pruitt-Igoe in St. Louis (the most infamous example) was torn down with much hullabaloo, but there are other Pruitt-Igoes in every major city in America, and the basic lesson remains unlearned.

There is another serious problem that we face in America. As is the case in other highly-developed countries, a lack of cohesion occurs in communities with highly mobile populations. This, coupled with high concentrations of people in metropolitan settings, has made much of our urban landscape antagonistic and unusable.

The questions that face us are two: can the architect-planner re-create the milieu and attributes of the single-family house in a setting 30 times as dense; and can the planner create new forms of community to replace the old, disappearing communities of ethnic uniformity?

Often when we think of residential environments, we think of the people who live in them as being of a uniform type: e.g., families raising children. That may have been true of previous generations when people had a short life span and lived in extended families—three or four generations together. These days, with increased social and physical mobility, longer life expectancies, government assumption of responsibility for the care of retired persons, and adult people living alone (or together) without children, we have a large variety of age and life-style groups, each demanding very different forms of residential environments.

We have tried, at the Institute for Community Design Analysis in New York, to come to some understanding of these variations in residential environments as a first step in coming to grips with the above two problems. We have marshalled data to support what most people intuitively know and feel anyway. But there is a difference between designing with something that you intuitively feel versus designing with information that has statistical support—information that comes from not only looking at residential environments but from watching people's behavior, recording vacancy rates, management costs, how people use space, asking people what they feel about where they live. When you work this way, you work with a degree of certainty. And you know that the environment that you will then produce will perform in an expected fashion. You can become an advocate for the needs of people, supported by an army of facts and experience.

Let us examine the existing patterns of ownership, use and feelings of responsibility that exist in different residential settings. Single-family houses, whether they are detached, semi-detached, or row houses, all have certain fundamental ingredients in common even though the density of each type is markedly different. Both the individual unit and the grounds around it are the environment of a particular family. They own it even if they only rent it. They own it from the moment they can dictate who can come into it, who uses it, what goes on in it. And this is true not only for the activity within the four walls of the building, but for the grounds on either side.

But when you increase the density and produce a walk-up building—and have six families sharing an entry, rather than one—you have created something radically new in the human residential environment. Internal space is no longer just private and assigned to individual families; you now have space within the envelope of a building that is shared by a group of families. The question of who may use that common circulation space and for what, and who takes care of it, now arises for the first time. Who has a right into that space, what activities are to be tolerated within it? Is throwing garbage on the floor possible? Is writing on the walls possible? If somebody makes a mess, who cleans it up? You have either to distribute such responsibility among the residents of the building or you have to appoint a guardian who represents all the residents to undertake such a duty.

Public   Private

Semi-public   Semi-private

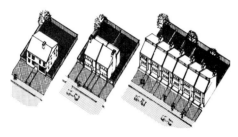

Single-family houses

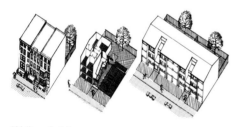

Walk-up buildings

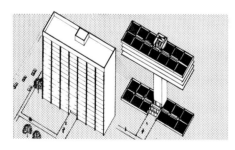

High-rise buildings

This is a very critical departure from the first form of building: the single-family house. It becomes particularly important where the people living in the environment do not have the funds available to hire or pay for a party who will represent them in cleaning and maintaining and guarding the entry to that particular building.

But when you are building at a higher density still, and instead of having six families sharing an entry you have 126, then the space inside is no longer semi-private, it's really public. It's public as a street is public: anybody has access to it. It's hard to distinguish who belongs, who doesn't, who is a resident, who is an intruder. It's hard to feel, when you are one of 126 families, one of 500 people, sharing that environment, that the corridor or elevator is meaningfully yours. And it's not surprising then, that the activities that take place there are uncontrolled and uncontrollable, that anybody and everybody has access to it, and that people withdraw to the confines of their own units which are at least private and which they control. The question is, who takes care of the rest of it?

Now we know of such environments that work, that are occupied by middle class residents and where no problem exists, because there are funds available for maintenance. They can assign someone the responsibility of controlling the public space. But in low-income housing, funds for that sort of thing—maintenance, security, preventive maintenance, cleaning—are not available.

There's a further problem: the lower the income of the people, the more intensively they use their home environment. They don't have the kinds of choices or options that are open to middle class and upper income people. Their kids do not go to gymnastics school or violin lessons or horseback riding or boating in the afternoon. There isn't money for that. The home environment is used thoroughly during the 24 hours and fully during the summer. You go to a public housing project at the end of a summer and it has been wrung out. It has been used to death. It becomes all the more important then, when you are designing an environment

for low-income people, to appreciate the intensity with which they use it and the importance it has in their day to day existence.

Now let's examine the environments of row houses, walk-ups and high rises at a larger scale to see the patterns they produce in cities and the consequences we face. If you look at a four-block area, you see that the row house is the private domain of its individual families. The front and backyards and even the sidewalk, which is in fact an extension of the dwelling, because there is no other dwelling sharing it, become semi-private spaces. The only thing that remains public is the throughway in the street. People who live in neighborhoods like this will even question whether the street is truly public. It is only public so long as a car is passing through it. Stop and you'll see that in fact it is not truly public. People have a proprietary attitude toward that space. They want to know what you are doing, why you stopped, who you are looking for. That space is yours to pass through but if you stay there you have to obey certain rules and decorum however undefined, however informal.

When you go to a high-rise environment, and the spaces within the building, the corridors, the lobbies, are already public, then the grounds are truly public and so of course are the streets. And the question then is, who in society will take care of this? Do we now have to hire a police force, and maintenance men to do the sorts of things that individuals would normally do if the environment were so subdivided that they could feel it was theirs? Whose failure is this? It is the failure of the architectural profession. I believe that it is partially our failure in that we have duped ourselves into believing that we were not creating dramatically different socio-physical environments. Instead of concerning ourselves with these differences we gave ourselves the problem of designing the facades of these environmental monstrosities. If you look at the solutions to high-rise living proposed by Le Corbusier, Peter and Alison Smithson, and Yamasaki, among others, they are merely facade solutions. If the internal space was manipulated in a complex fashion it is only to produce a more interesting facade—not a more useful living environment.

**The Location of Housing Crime in Relation to Building Height
(Reported Felonies per 1,000 Families)**

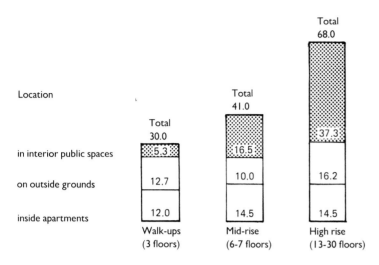

Source: N.Y.C. Housing Authority data 1967:N = 87.[13]

The Assignment of Family Types to Building Types

Family Type	Building Types					
	1. Single-family	2. Walk-ups	3. Medium High Rise		4. Elevator High Rise	
			Doorman	Non-Doorman	Doorman	Non-Doorman
Families with children	**	**	*	●	●	■
Elderly	*	■	**	*	**	*
Working adults	■	●	**	■	**	■

** strongly recommended
 * recommended

● barely acceptable
■ not recommended

Some years ago, the staff of our institute determined that if we could demonstrate that crime against people—crime against property—was one of the things that was being affected by poorly designed environments, we could convince the government to change its housing policies. We thought this would be more effective than demonstrating that existing housing is not a useful environment in which to raise kids. It's much easier to talk to government about felony rate than about satisfied people—much more effective. So that's why we searched out some crime variables. And of course, the crime pattern increases dramatically when you go from walk-up to medium-rise to high-rise housing. And it's in those communally held spaces that become increasingly public and uncontrolled and unusable that the most dramatic increases in crime occur. We were able to predict 67 percent of the variation in instability through those independent variables—burglary and fear—and 65 percent through experience of personal crime rate. And every one of the independent variables—the use of space, social interaction and residents' control of space—was measured by how people actually use the environment: how they identify with it, what they would do in certain situations. All this helped show that, in fact, the design of an environment can determine how people will behave in those private and semi-private and public spaces, how they will interact with others, what they think of themselves and their rights in such places. This in turn affects their fears, the actual burglary and crime rate within the building and their willingness to remain in residence, as measured by the vacancy rate and the turnover rate within the building.

I am seeking a role for the architectural profession that will allow it to begin to serve society in much the same way that the medical society dictates public health standards. I'm talking about our becoming important to society as advocates of basic mental and physical health standards.

Further conclusions of our study indicate that high rises for families with children are clearly undesirable, but high rises for elderly—if it is a building limited totally to the elderly—can be very satisfactory indeed. Similarly, single people and couples without children find high-rise buildings produce very desirable residential environments. Families with many children, however, perform best in a single-family house on its own piece of land: it may only be a row house if density and cost are critical factors. Families with one child or a couple of very young children might even be able to survive in a two- or three-story walk-up building for a few years.

Another social phenomenon of great importance to our work is the disappearance of the extended family—the consequence of a highly mobile, post-industrial society. The equivalent of our entire country's population moves every five years. Young people move off to college, or where the opportunities are, and rarely come back. The concept of the extended family, the ethnic enclave surrounding a factory or market, is gone and gone forever. The small town environment is gone too, and some will say, "Thank God!" because they see the opportunities within the large cities and restrictions are usually within the small towns that are overburdened with tight social structures. But we pay a price for this freedom and that price is the disappearance of the extended family.

The question is: can we create a facsimile, a substitute for the extended family in contemporary society? The nuclear family unit fighting it out by itself, whether it's a family with children, elderly, a single person or a couple, just can't make it on its own. It's too rough a place out there—our modern city. One of the things that we concluded from our examination of environments is that today's extended family equivalent in the urban setting is the group of similar age and life style in a shared environment. Such extended families sharing a communal interest need not consist of large, segregated enclaves; they can be groupings of no more than 150 to 250 people. And they can be placed adjacent to groupings of other, different life styles to create urban (or even neighborhood) heterogeneity. So that one type of development—say a high-rise complex if you will, for elderly—can be located immediately adjacent to a walk-up complex or to row houses for families with children and that, in turn, adjacent to an apartment building of some sort for working singles and couples. Once you begin to group people by life style (based on their ages and the activities they pursue) you can also begin to provide community space that serves their particular needs—to provide the amalgam that brings them together—something you cannot do if you have a conflict of life styles and communal interests. We have also noticed that differences in race and income between people are not as noticeable, do not become as much of an issue, if people are grouped by similarity in age and life style. Often, what is perceived as a conflict between racial groups is little more than a conflict between age groups. People think it's white against black when it's really white elderly trying very hard to live with black families with children and coming into a conflict over the use of a common residential environment. Grouping people by similarity of life style reduces differences in race and income group; the differences become smaller, more marginal, less important.

Our institute was asked to design a moderate-income housing development for Newark, New Jersey. We were given a program of 316 units, 46 percent elderly, 18 percent families with two or more older children, and 36 percent families with one child or two youngsters. Although we could have created a mix of units of various sizes in one building type and repeated the building type throughout the site, we determined that three different building types were needed, each to accommodate a different kind of group. The architect can either create environments in which people will interact comfortably and assume social and communal responsibilities, or he can create environments in which people withdraw to the privacy of their own apartments, avoiding contact and social commitments with their neighbors. The architect can also create a new form of extended family and use it as a vehicle not only for providing more satisfactory commercial space, but as a vehicle to facilitate racial and economic integration.

But to play such a role the architect-planner must learn to lead rather than to be led. Often a developer will say to an architect: "Give me a building that is a mix of 30 percent efficiencies, 30 percent one-bedroom units, 30 percent two-bedroom units, and 10 percent three-bedroom units," so that he can have a range of apartments to rent, because that's the market out there. Such distributions may represent the overall market, but as a microcosm it represents a difficult building for people to live in. Such a mix does not have to be provided within a single building but can be provided in the larger macrocosm, in a wide variety of building types each tailored to the needs of specific groups to a community of interest.

Before the Architects

Kusakabe Kimbei
Workmen's Holiday 1890s
albumen print
Collection Lawrence and Martha Friedricks

● *Bernard Rudofsky*

Non-pedigreed architecture is no longer the vaguely perceived subject it was 50-odd years ago. Once the sole province of anthropologists and ethnologists, it now counts aficionados even among architects, and the protests and vituperations that greeted *Architecture Without Architects* in 1964 have gradually faded away.

The first inkling that alien kinds of shelter might be relevant to our architecture came with the rediscovery of the Japanese house in the wake of the Pacific War. Its striking aesthetic qualities caught our imagination no less than the life style it imposed on the inhabitant. However, just when we thought we had stumbled upon a treasure trove of Oriental know-how, the Japanese repudiated their traditional ways in favor of Western ones, which greatly strengthened our belief that we know best and have nothing to learn from others.

Our early distrust of alien domestic architecture is not difficult to understand. Modern architecture's prophets and pioneers, whose doctrines went unchallenged for many years, were almost invariably men of parochial mind, untraveled and loath to venture beyond their drawing boards. Their foremost aim was to homogenize the world of architecture by impressing upon it a vapid "international style." Enamored of mechanization, they considered people who mainly depended on the utilization of sun, wind and waterpower embarrassingly primitive.

Although we eventually went through some changes of heart and mind in matters of architecture, nothing points to changes for the better in our customs and usages. How do patterns of living and architecture intersect? The two ought to complement each other, but we must examine our patterns of living to verify that assumption.

There is all the difference in the world between getting acquainted with a foreign culture through book reading and sightseeing, and from living abroad by one's wits. The latter has nothing to do with voyeurism, romance or desertion. It merely disabuses us of the notion that the civilization we are born into is the only true and saving one.

I'll examine some tangible aspects of domestic architecture, and try to perform a partial autopsy of the house, and discuss the findings in the plainest of terms. Let us begin at the bottom and consider the house's floor. The floor is, literally and figuratively, the touchstone of a civilization. A good floor is much more than a delight to the eye; it appeals to that most sensuous of our senses, touch. Anyone who has walked barefoot on a polished marble floor, on tatami, or on those soft layers of carpet in the rooms of a Near Eastern house, has a better grasp of Oriental languor than can be gleaned from reading an unexpurgated edition of the *Arabian Nights*.

Wooden bathtub for two with
a view of the sea
Atami, Japan

By way of contrast, a recent newspaper notice, calling attention to the vandalism perpetrated at White House receptions, found the spectacle of "hundreds of spike heels digging into irreplaceable rugs so appalling that invitations ought to say something about heels." A trivial matter? Not to my mind.

There simply is no getting around the fact that we are not housebroken. At the White House, guests from every part of the world have an opportunity to assess the cultural peculiarities of their hosts. Rugs, like tatami, are not meant to be walked upon with shoes. Yet men balk at the suggestion to take them off, afraid of compromising their manliness, while women believe that their shoes are an integral part of their charms. Even the most zealous feminists conform, although high heels are the classical symbol of bondage.

Once, while spending a year in the 50th state, I noticed that workmen and tradespeople who came to my house always left their footwear at the door—without being asked to do so—and so did my guests, whether Orientals or Occidentals. I concluded that the proximity of the Far East has imbued these islanders with a love of cleanliness that on the mainland is considered downright un-American.

Over here, cleanliness has its limitations. Take that miscarriage of domesticity, that sordid room we call bathroom. The very word is a misnomer—at best, a euphemism—applied to what actually is a privy with a tub. This tub is a caricature of the real thing, yet it suits those who never had a chance to get acquainted with any other kind. "People are happy," wrote Aldous Huxley, "they get what they want, and never what they can't get." Innocent as we are of a bathing culture, we *wash* in the tub, a habit Easterners look upon with distaste and disgust. "In India," says Santha Rama Rau, "the people consider an ordinary tub bath an extraordinarily dirty habit. The thought of sitting in one's own soiled water is altogether revolting to them." The custom of washing outside the

tub, that is, *before* entering it, to us seems paradoxical, not to say perverse. But then, the essence of cleanliness escapes us because, although we broke away from the worst aberrations of puritanism, we hardly are on intimate terms with our bodies.

Today, it is the lower regions of the body that are in the dog house. To wit, only the most pretentious bathroom has provision for washing privy parts after emptying bowels and bladder—in other words, a bidet. To the nation the bidet symbolizes the inherent wickedness of personal hygiene. The very sound of the word is as shocking as the word "leg" was to our great grandparents. Sporadically manufactured in the U.S., today the bidet is touted as a status symbol, an article for "the ultra-sophisticated." The appliance that has *no* business in our so-called bathroom is the toilet; it certainly should be in a separate compartment. To defecate in the bathroom is as repulsive to the fastidious as to defecate in any other room. The prisoner in his cell has no choice. We do.

In my recent exhibition on the unknown art of living I reconstructed a Japanese Great Convenience Place, or what novelist Tanizaki called "the most poetic spot in the Japanese house." This is not the place to go into lyrical description of the Japanese privy; suffice it to say that Orientals and Occidentals differ in their elimination posture: they squat, we sit. On the honest-to-goodness oriental john there is no seat. Does sitting on the toilet make us civilized? If anything, it makes us constipated. Every physician worth his salt will admit that squatting is the only correct posture for defecation, although he is far from following his own advice.

French 18th-century bidet
carved fruitwood, caning, leather
and glazed earthenware
Collection Cooper-Hewitt Museum,
New York

The unhealthiness of the toilet seat differs only by degrees from that of its cousin, the chair. In Asian and African houses, chairs are almost entirely absent. People are floor-sitters by preference, and not, as we like to believe, because of poverty. Even in a hybrid civilization as today's Japan, the tired businessman on returning home, seeks to recharge his ebbing vitality by settling down on the matted floor of what usually is the only Japanese room in his Western-style house.

A review of domestic architecture in the eastern half of the world—all the way from the Bosporus to the end of China—discloses chairless seating arrangements hardly known hereabouts. Dais and divan, the Chinese platform—prototype of couch, bed and table—are preferable to Western sitting contraptions on several counts. For the "comfort" derived from a chair's support is based on nothing more than consent. Need for support, whether to bolster one's self-esteem, or to uphold a crumbling spine, reveals a fundamental weakness of our nature and, ever since we came to depend on so-called comfort, we turned it, by some mental conjuring, into a mark of superiority. Backache, a crippling ailment which affects four out of five Americans is primarily a disease of Western-style living. Neither surgery nor drugs will cure it. And how come nobody noticed the intrinsic *ugliness* of the chair? Our commercially conditioned ideas of the useful and the beautiful are rarely substantiated by facts.

If our non-bathroom betrays pathetic misconceptions of personal hygiene, the bedroom exemplifies our ineptness to turn space to good use. Most people who plan to build a house try to enclose a maximum of space with a minimum of expense. Alas, by the time they move into their new quarters, a good deal of the precious space is taken up by beds. Once upon a time beds may have been the bedrock of a happy marriage but to judge from today's divorce statistics, they have lost their magic power. Still, beds are indispensable in countries whose inhabitants never made culture contact with clean floors. Future generations will look back uncomprehendingly at the waste of space caused by our sleeping habits. For, if we had any *savoir-dormir,* a bedroom with its bedsteads and bedside tables would strike us as no less anachronistic than our great grandparents' parlor.

In order to keep our slender hold on sanity and dignity, we must turn our thoughts into new avenues. The house of man has to become again an instrument for living, instead of a machine for living. This would make all the difference—like between playing a violin and playing a jukebox. A sensibly conceived house would abrogate the need for an escape into the infantile world of packaged entertainment and the senile one of hobbies. In order to nudge our imagination, we ought to *build* a house based on the combined know-how of mankind in the field of domestic architecture—a house that would incorporate not only desirable amenities of past and present life styles, but that radiates the sensuousness that more enlightened people than we were able to impart to *their* houses.

Emilio Ambasz
Working in New York and Bologna, Emilio Ambasz is a practicing architect and industrial designer. He has taught at Princeton University and the Carnegie Institute of Technology and was Curator of Design at The Museum of Modern Art, New York, for several years. He is the author of:

Italy: The New Domestic Landscape. New York: The Museum of Modern Art, 1972.

The Taxi Project: Realistic Solutions for Today. New York: The Museum of Modern Art, 1976.

Stuart Cohen
A Chicago-based architect, Stuart Cohen has taught at the University of Illinois, Chicago Circle Campus. He is Chicago correspondent for *Progressive Architecture* magazine, and the author of:

"Physical Context/Cultural Context: Including It All." *Oppositions 2.* 1974.

Chicago Architects: A Revisionist View of Chicago Architecture. Athens, Ohio: Swallow Press, 1976.

Grant Hildebrand
Professor of architecture and art history at the University of Washington, Seattle, Grant Hildebrand is the author of:

Designing for Industry: The Architecture of Albert Kahn. Cambridge, Mass.: MIT Press, 1974.

Ralph Knowles
Professor of architecture at the University of Southern California, Ralph Knowles is the author of:

Energy and Form: An Ecological Approach to Urban Growth. Cambridge, Mass.: MIT Press, 1978.

"Solar Access and Urban Form." *AIA Journal.* February, 1980.

Sun, Rhythm and Form. Cambridge, Mass.: MIT Press, forthcoming.

Spiro Kostof
Professor of architectural history at the University of California, Berkeley, Spiro Kostof organized the exhibition *The Third Rome: 1870–1950 Traffic and Glory,* for the University Art Museum, Berkeley. He wrote the catalogue for that exhibition and is also the author of:

The Caves of God: The Monastic Environment of Byzantine Cappodocia. Cambridge: MIT Press, 1972

The Architect: Chapters in the History of a Profession. New York: Oxford University Press, 1976.

Charles Moore
A Los Angeles-based architect and former Dean of the Yale School of Architecture, Charles Moore is Professor of Architecture at the School of Architecture, University of California, Los Angeles, and the author of:

The Place of Houses (with Gerald Allen and Donlyn Lyndon). New York: Holt, Rinehart and Winston, 1974.

"After a New Architecture: The Best Shape for a Chimera." *Oppositions 3.* 1974.

Dimensions: Space, Scale and Shape in Architecture (with Gerald Allen). New York: Architectural Record Books, 1976.

Body, Memory and Architecture (with Kent Bloomer). New Haven, Conn.: Yale University Press, 1977.

Oscar Newman
President and founder of the Institute for Community Design Analysis, a non-profit research corporation engaged in the study of the effects of environmental design on human behavior, Oscar Newman is also a practicing architect and urban planner. He is the author of:

Defensible Space: Crime Prevention Through Urban Design. New York: Macmillan, 1972.

Community of Interest. Garden City, New York: Doubleday, 1980.

Bernard Rudofsky
An architect, engineer, and world traveler, Bernard Rudofsky recently guest curated the exhibition *Now I Lay Me Down to Eat* at the Cooper-Hewitt Museum. He is the author of:

Streets for People. Garden City, New York: Doubleday, 1969.

Architecture without Architects. Garden City, New York: Doubleday, 1969.

The Prodigious Builders. New York: Harcourt, Brace, Jovanovich, 1979.

Now I Lay Me Down to Eat: Notes and Footnotes on the Lost Art of Living. Garden City, New York: Doubleday, 1980.

Special thanks to Margaret O'Neill-Ligon who assisted with research, manuscript preparation and illustrations for this issue.

DQ congratulates James H. Timberlake of the office of Venturi, Rauch and Scott Brown, Philadelphia, on his recent Rome Prize Fellowship. His illustrations for the Hennepin Avenue project discussed in *Design Quarterly 117* were a valuable addition to the issue, and we failed to properly credit the drawings.